DAVID WILLIAMSON'S

THE GREAT DIVIDE

CURRENCY PRESS
The performing arts publisher

CURRENT THEATRE SERIES

First published in 2024
by Currency Press
Gadigal Land, Suite 310, 46–56 Kippax Street, Surry Hills, NSW 2010, Australia
enquiries@currency.com.au
www.currency.com.au

in association with Ensemble Theatre

Reprinted 2025.

Typeset by Brighton Gray for Currency Press.
Printed by Fineline Print + Copy Services, Revesby, NSW.
Cover image shows Georgie Parker and Kate Raison. Cover image by Brett Boardman
Cover design by Alphabet Studio.

Currency Press acknowledges the Traditional Owners of the Country on which we live and work. We pay our respects to all Aboriginal and Torres Strait Islander Elders, past and present.

A catalogue record for this book is available from the National Library of Australia

Contents

The Great Divide 1

Theatre Program at the end of the playtext

The Great Divide was first produced by Ensemble Theatre, Cammeraigal Country, Kirribilli, on 8 March 2024, with the following cast:

RACHEL POULTER	Caitlyn Burley
PENNY POULTER	Emma Diaz
BRIAN / JOEL	James Lugton
ALEX WHITTLE	Georgie Parker
GRACE DELAHUNTY	Kate Raison
ALAN BRIDGER	John Wood

Director, Mark Kilmurry
Assistant Director, Julia Robertson
Set and Costume Designer, James Browne
Lighting Designer, Veronique Benett
Sound Designer, Daryl Wallis
Stage Manager, Erin Shaw
Assistant Stage Manager, Alexis Worthing
Costume Supervisor, Renata Beslik

CHARACTERS

ALEX WHITTLE
GRACE DELAHUNTY
ALAN BRIDGER
PENNY POULTER
JOEL
BRIAN
RACHEL POULTER

This play text went to press before the end of rehearsals and may differ from the play as performed.

ALEX WHITTLE *waits impatiently in the conference room of Wallis Heads council chambers. Standing in the background is her personal assistant* GRACE DELAHUNTY. ALEX *is power-dressed with an expensive necklace of pearls.* GRACE *is also in her fifties and has been PA to* ALEX *for years.* GRACE *is dressed in brown and beige.* ALEX *looks at her watch and frowns.* ALAN, *a businessman in a suit in his late fifties, approaches.* ALEX *stands and they greet and shake hands.* ALEX *turns to* GRACE.

ALEX: Grace, this is the Mayor of Wallis Heads, Alan Bridger. Alan, this is my assistant Grace.

ALEX *sees that* GRACE *has pulled out a notebook and a pen. She signals impatiently to* GRACE *to put the notebook away.*

[*Sharply*] Grace, off the record!

GRACE *hastily puts the notebook back into her handbag.*

GRACE: Sorry.

ALEX: [*to* ALAN] So let's see it.

ALAN *opens his computer and presses keys and on a large screen at the back of the room we see a replay of a recent current affairs interview.*

The interview opens with a shot of PENNY POULTER, *in her mid-thirties, a feisty woman who doesn't mince words, who stands in front of partially cleared and attractive bushland.*

JOEL: Mrs Poulter, I believe you've started a petition protesting against the shire council's recent action.

PENNY: Yeah.

JOEL: Why is that?

PENNY: Because I'm bloody ropeable. Look at that land behind me. Earmarked in the town plan as future social housing, so what does our council do? Sell it to Australia's richest woman so she can turn it into a golf course. And they've thrown in the land next to the course that was going to be public park so she can build sixty luxury residences and turn it into an exclusive country club and make a huge profit.

JOEL: It's planned to be a first-class championship course.

PENNY: Twenty thousand dollars to join? Two hundred dollars a round?

JOEL: The council view is that it will attract high-end tourists and wealthy retirees and substantially boost the town economy.

PENNY: So what happens to me and all the rest of us who aren't 'high end', but've spent most of our lives here?

JOEL: The council claims that property values will increase substantially and the net worth of our homeowners will soar.

PENNY: Half the town rents! What happens to us when rents soar?

JOEL: Council admits that life could be more difficult for some, but the overall benefits to the shire will be overwhelmingly positive. Alex Whittle is paying the shire thirty million dollars for the land.

PENNY: None of that thirty million is going to community facilities. It's all earmarked for grand new council chambers that would give the Taj Mahal a run for its money!

JOEL: The council has made a decision they feel is in the greater interest of all ratepayers.

PENNY: Not ratepayers like me. And there are plenty of us. Which is why I'm starting a petition to get our present council of pro-development shonks voted out at the upcoming elections and get us a council that really does act in the interests of the Wallis Heads I know and love.

JOEL: Thank you, Penny Poulter.

The interview ends. There's a silence. When ALEX *speaks she's angry.*

ALEX: Alan, I was told you were an astute political operator.

ALAN: I like to think so.

ALEX: When I come into town, and the first thing I see is myself being trashed on your local screens by your local version of Jacqui Lambie, Whisky Tango Foxtrot am I supposed to think?

ALAN: It was unfortunate—

ALEX: It's a fucking PR disaster! Can you please explain how she got to know top-secret information only you and your council are supposed to know?

ALAN: We're baffled.

ALEX: Could I hazard a guess. One of your councillors had too much to drink, and couldn't help big noting himself, and now we have

Little Miss Nobody spilling it on prime-time local television. Who the hell is she?

ALAN: A single mother who stacks shelves in the supermarket.

ALEX: Why did they interview her?

ALAN: She wrote a very strong, and I have to say, well-written letter to the local paper.

ALEX: Is your local media so hungry for controversy that every loud-mouthed little nimpty numpty is handed a soapbox? No wonder democracy is headed for extinction. Is any more of what we're planning coming out?

ALAN: It won't. I've read the riot act to the council.

ALEX: They'd better listen because if there's any more of this I'm out of here. There are other options on my list.

ALAN: We're all strongly behind this, Alex.

ALEX: You said in your last email there were some worries. What worries?

ALAN: That if any more gets out before the elections there could be a backlash.

ALEX: If your bloody council can keep their mouths shut there won't. Then as soon as you're all re-elected you greenlight everything.

ALAN: There might need to be some debate.

ALEX: I don't do debate, Alan. Debate means nothing ever happens. If your council can't deliver me what I need then Wallis Heads can keep on being the sad, dying, dumbass little backwater it is.

ALAN: I wouldn't quite call it that.

ALEX: Then go and have another look at the shops down the main street and count the 'For Lease' signs. Look at your young kids lining up for buses to get them out of here because there aren't any jobs!

ALAN: We all want that to change, Alex, but Penny Poulter is getting lots of signatures and I'm just warning you there is a chance we won't be re-elected.

ALEX: A supermarket shelf-stacker? Wearing Crocs on camera? This is not exactly a fearsome adversary.

ALAN: There's talk that she and the Greenies are getting together a ticket.

ALEX: No-one's going to vote in a pack of lunatics who think wobble-throated reed warblers are more important than their own bloody species!

ALAN: I'm just saying that, now that your golf course is out in the open, our re-election isn't a lay-down misère.

ALEX: More money for your campaign? Is that what you're saying? Fine. I'll spend what it takes.

ALAN: There's a problem there too. We have to declare where our funding comes from.

ALEX: [*with disbelief at his naivety*] Alan, it won't be coming from me. It'll be coming from a local citizens' group who support progress.

ALAN: What group?

ALEX: Organise one!

ALAN: That's perilously close to being illegal.

ALEX: Alan, even if it is it'll take fifteen years of appeals before they can prove it is, then we just pay the pitiful fine and all's well with the world.

[*Off his worried look*] You're not exactly a man of steel are you?

ALAN: I'm just warning you. There's a lot of chatter on social media.

ALEX: Saying what?

ALAN: 'Golf for the wealthy and the rest of us can go to hell' kind of stuff.

ALEX: What do they think? Every deadbeat without a cent is entitled to tee-off on a world-class golf course for nix?

ALAN: All I'm trying to say is things have got more complicated.

ALEX: Alan, I'm guessing you popped out of the womb with a frown on your face.

ALAN: There's quite a bit of anti-Alex Whittle feeling around already. 'She can't come in here and do what she likes,' kind of thing.

ALEX: They don't want their property values to skyrocket? They object to their net worth increasing threefold? Are you kidding me?

ALAN: As Penny noted, a lot of our population are renters and they're worried about rent increases.

ALEX: There will be rent increases for God's sake. Big ones. Those who can no longer afford to live here go elsewhere. Market forces. That's how the world works.

ALAN: The council understands the reality of the market, but for those adversely affected—

ALEX: Alan, the world owes no-one a living. There are winners and losers. Always were, always will be. I'm trying to turn this into a town for winners.

ALAN: Alex, we've got to bring the town with us. You're already seen by some as—

ALEX: What?

ALAN: Driven.

ALEX: And?

ALAN: Ruthless?

ALEX: And?

ALAN: Arrogant.

ALEX: How wrong they all are. They will shortly see the real me.

ALAN: Who is?

ALEX: Compassionate. Caring. Doing what I love best. Helping local kids doing it tough. Karen, the young soccer whizz whose dad's battling cancer. Little Debbie, the dancer whose single mum can't afford ballet shoes. Shane, the young musician with an alcoholic dad who can't afford a good guitar.

ALAN: I'm a bit uneasy with that sort of thing.

ALEX: A foundation that'll help a lot of kids? What's not to like? We just need to find a cracker of a kid with media appeal to kick things off.

ALAN: Alex …

ALEX: What? What's worrying you, Alan?

ALAN: It seems a tad … manipulative.

ALEX: A tad? It's totally manipulative. Alan, what kind of planet do you think you're living on? Ever since social media image is everything. We live in a Kardashian world. Young idiots cavort cutely on TikTok and become millionaire influencers overnight. You either join the game or go under.

ALAN: Yes but—

ALEX: Check out your own Facebook page, Alan. I've never seen a more airbrushed family. Your little grandkid Leo. He has to have had intensive cuteness coaching. Who taught your dog to smile? Don't pretend you're not into the game as much as any of us.

ALAN: Yes, but—

ALEX: Alan, you're starting to worry me. If my main backers go jellyfish on me I'm out of here.

ALAN: Jellyfish? You don't get to be a senior sergeant in the Queensland Police force without learning which heads to kick. We're with you, Alex. All the way. But Penny Poulter is dogged.

ALEX: Alan, she is a supermarket shelf-stacker! Talk about a nervous Nellie.

ALAN: She's well known. People like her.

ALEX: I'll deal with her. And you'll all get re-elected. Okay?

ALAN: Okay.

ALEX: Just keep a hellish tight lid on the other things we're planning and all will be fine.

He nods, hesitates and leaves. ALEX *turns to* GRACE.

Grace, do some research around town. Find me my first young future champion.

GRACE: I'll try.

ALEX: [*flaring*] Grace, you know what the most irritating words in the English language are? 'I'll try!' And I'm hearing it from you more and more often. You're not paid to try! You're paid to do! Talk to headmasters, sporting clubs, rotary club, chamber of commerce, local drama groups, whatever. Just find me my first worthy candidate and in a hurry.

GRACE *nods. Then moves to go.*

Oh and Grace. Arrange a meeting with this two-bit agitator. What's her name again?

GRACE: Penny. Penny Poulter.

ALEX: Get her here as soon as possible. One meeting is all it usually needs to have them running for cover.

GRACE *turns to go.*

[*Fossicking in the cupboard*] You were supposed to iron my suit. It looks like it's gone three times through a wood chipper.

GRACE: I rang the front desk and they said they don't have any irons.

ALEX: Grace, have you ever heard the word initiative, because if you have you obviously don't know what it means!

ALEX *picks up the phone.*

Front desk? Get me the manager. You are the manager? Good. This is Alex Whittle in the so called 'presidential' suite. You apparently haven't got an iron, right? Well here's the deal. Go and buy one and have it in this room in half an hour or I will buy this flea-bitten hotel and the first thing I'll do is sack you!

She hangs up and looks at GRACE.

Right?

GRACE: Alex, be fair. There's no way I could've done that.

ALEX: No, but you could have pointed out that you work for the most powerful woman in the country and that paying fifty dollars for a new iron could prove a very sensible investment. No?

GRACE: I could've been more assertive.

ALEX: Yes you could've. And this room?

[*Indicating around her with disgust*] Is this the best you could do?

GRACE: It is—

ALEX: It's freaking me out! It's the exact same wallpaper as the funeral parlour that laid out Grandma!

GRACE: It is a little tired.

ALEX: Tired? They've used the same interior decorator who invented fluffy toilet-seat covers. And as well as that it's way too small, the basin plug sticks, and the mattress is so soft I feel like I'm back in my mother's bloody womb! You should bloody well know by now that if you punch my mattress and your knuckles don't hurt it's not hard enough.

GRACE: I missed the plug. And I forgot to punch the mattress. Sorry, Alex.

ALEX: This hotel can't be the best in town, surely?

GRACE: There is a state room, or so-called state room at the Mountford Hotel downtown.

ALEX: Is it bigger? Not so tired?

GRACE: It's bigger and its decor could possibly pass for twenty-first century, but it looks out on the main street and I know how you hate noise.

ALEX: I hate poky rooms even more. Change hotels as soon as possible and try and get it right next time, Grace. And that eleven o'clock call from Gavin and Joe? What happened to that?

GRACE: You told me to reschedule everything for the next couple of days.

ALEX: Good God, Grace. Sometimes I wonder what the hell I was doing when I put you on the payroll. I'm on the point of closing a deal with those guys. A big deal. I thought you'd have enough brains to realise that. Get them on Zoom as soon as possible and get that … what's her name again?

GRACE: Penny. Penny Poulter.

ALEX: Get her but only when I'm in the new hotel. She'd scarcely be impressed with this rabbit hutch, would she?

GRACE: I'm sorry about that, Alex. I was tossing up between the two rooms but I thought the noise factor …

ALEX: Grace, why do you think kings erect magnificent palaces? To signal who they are and the power they wield. Did you honestly think that anyone I met in this shithole would be impressed?

GRACE: The state room in the Mountford is only marginally more impressive.

ALEX: Which is exactly what's wrong with this fucking place. The most beautiful little piece of undeveloped coastline on the Eastern Seaboard and it's still in a time warp.

GRACE *turns to go, but* ALEX *hasn't finished.*

Grace, I've achieved a lot in my life. Do you know why?

GRACE: You work hard.

ALEX: So does the kid who delivers Uber Eats but he's never going to be rich. I am what I am because I see opportunities that others don't. And more often than not those opportunities are obvious, but the majority of humanity just doesn't bother to look. But I do and it's not rocket science. All you need is intelligence and foresight and a great personal assistant, but at the moment I have to say that I'm worried about that last essential, Grace. You booked the wrong room in the wrong hotel, didn't check the details and cancelled the wrong meeting. How long have you been with me now?

GRACE: Seventeen-and-three-quarter years.

ALEX: I'd hate to have to let you go, but please understand that performance outweighs sentiment when you're running a complex business empire like I am. I mean it. I would hate to have to let you go, so for my sake as well as yours, please try and smarten up.

GRACE: I will, Alex. I will.

GRACE *turns to go but as she approaches the door there's a knock. She opens it and takes an iron from the person on the other side and thanks her.* ALEX *nods her head as if to say, 'See. It's not that hard.'*

So, your suit or the talent quest?

ALEX: Go find my kid, but make sure you're back in time to do the suit before we go out and endure whatever miserable cuisine this town has to offer. What have you booked?

GRACE: The best seem to be the Leong Dong Palace—

ALEX: The what?

GRACE: Spelt L-E-O-N-G.

ALEX: And Dong spelt D-O-N-G I presume. Good God, what's the other?

GRACE: Italian. L'Ultima Cena which apparently means 'The Last Supper'.

ALEX: For fuck's sake find a Hungry Jack's.

GRACE *puts the iron down, nods and goes.* ALEX *waits until she's gone then picks up her phone.*

Richard? I have to let Grace go. She's making too many mistakes. Get our head-hunters looking for a top-quality replacement. Yes, regrettable but necessary, but there's no room for sentiment when a crucial mistake could cost us millions of dollars.

ALEX *ends the call and starts scrolling through her incoming emails.*

BRIAN, *the editor of the local newspaper, in his early fifties, and* ALAN *wait in Brian's office.*

ALAN: Brian, why in God's name are you giving the Poulter woman oxygen? I thought you wanted Alex's plans to go ahead?

BRIAN: I do. I also own the town newspaper and Penny's petition is causing a stir.

ALAN: Well it's going to cause a bigger stir if you interview her.

BRIAN: I've asked you both here so you can both put your points of view.

ALAN: You're giving her oxygen.

BRIAN: It's news, Alan. It's what I do.

ALAN *sighs.* PENNY *comes in without knocking.*

ALAN: You said you'd be here fifteen minutes ago.

PENNY: Some of us can't do whatever they want, whenever they want. Neil the Nazi ordered me to finish stacking the muesli shelves before I left.

BRIAN: You did tell us five-thirty would be fine.

PENNY: It would've been if I hadn't been forced to do unpaid overtime.

BRIAN: What I'm after is a calm discussion between the two of you. Do you mind if I record this?

PENNY: Fine.

ALAN: [*reluctantly*] Fine.

BRIAN: Penny, in a recent interview you used some pretty harsh adjectives about our council.

ALAN: You called us pro-development shonks.

PENNY: I was on television so I had to be polite.

BRIAN: Penny, I was hoping this would be more than just name calling.

PENNY: Look what Alan and his council have done. Sell off land earmarked for social housing! So that millionaires can belt the bejesus out of a little white ball and chat on about their share portfolios. Until then I was feeling at least hopeful because I was pretty high up on the social housing waiting list. I thought I had a chance of finally getting off the treadmill of paying nearly half my income in rent and starting to live a life where I don't have to count every bloody cent, then suddenly—pffft. Dream on, sucker.

ALAN: Penny, we offered really good tax-break deals to developers to take on social housing but got absolutely no interest.

PENNY: You didn't even try and ask for state government assistance.

ALAN: There's no pork barrel unless we're in a swinging seat and we aren't.

PENNY: You could have tried. The hopes of a lot of people in town were bound up that scheme which you lot promised to deliver.

BRIAN: I can understand your disappointment, but—

ALAN: Penny, you don't need to spend the rest of your life stacking supermarket shelves. I'm told that you topped your class at school every year.

PENNY: I did, then I made the mistake of believing my boyfriend when he said he wouldn't get me pregnant, which was my own stupid fault.

BRIAN: But now that young Rachel is a teenager you could go back and get qualified for something better.

PENNY: And what do Rachel and I live on while I'm taking three or four years getting some kind of qualification that'll be of any use?

Look, let's get real. My work is shit, but I'm lucky enough to live in a beautiful coastal town and I have lots of good friends and up to now I at least lived in hope, because I believed your promise that social housing was on its way. Now in an instant you've taken away that hope and handed the town we all love to a predator like Alex Whittle.

ALAN: Scarcely a predator. She donates a lot of money to deserving sporting organisations all over the country.

BRIAN: Alex's generosity is credited with two extra Australian gold medals at the last Olympics.

PENNY: Which put us one ahead of Holland. Those poor Dutch people will never bloody recover.

ALAN: Belittle her all you like, but most of the town will benefit greatly from this sale.

PENNY: Benefit? How are people like me going to benefit? Gather at sunset, hearts full of civic pride as we watch the sun sink behind thirty million dollars' worth of your shiny new council chambers. Which should have been a public swimming pool or community centre.

BRIAN: I asked you both here for a reasoned debate.

PENNY: Why would I bother? There's no way Alan and his development-mad crazies will ever change their mind. This is a waste of my time. I could've got three more signatures.

PENNY *gets up and walks out.* ALAN *and* BRIAN *look at each other.*

ALAN: Are you really going to print any of that?

BRIAN *sighs.*

BRIAN: It seemed like a good idea at the time.

PENNY *is sitting at her kitchen table looking furious. Her seventeen-year-old daughter* RACHEL, *in a school uniform, breezes in, a school satchel on her back which she sheds.* RACHEL *is athletic and hyperactive.*

PENNY: Where the hell have you been?

RACHEL: Waves are cranking off the point.

PENNY: What did you promise me?

RACHEL: Waves like today come once a month. Perfect shape, nearly two metres. Corduroy right out to the horizon. Amazing. Four-hundred-metre rides.

PENNY: What did you promise me?

RACHEL: Mum, I'm the state number two. I'm not just some little grommet.

PENNY: Homework?

RACHEL: Stop bloody obsessing about it. I'll bloody do it.

PENNY: I have to face your teachers every parents' night. Do you think it's fun to hear your daughter's rude, disruptive, and on track to fail her final year?

RACHEL: Mum, the stuff they teach is useless shit. I don't give a stuff about Hannibal and his bloody elephants.

PENNY: You said you wanted to learn about the ancient world.

RACHEL: You told me it was interesting.

PENNY: It was when I studied it.

RACHEL: Well it isn't now.

PENNY: Honey, the history of the ancient world hasn't changed all that much in eighteen-odd years. This is your final year! If you don't buckle down and study, you'll never get the marks to get into any decent course at university.

RACHEL: I don't want to go to university.

PENNY: You really think you can make it as a professional surfer?

RACHEL: Number two in the state in my age group?

PENNY: You're good. I'm proud. I really am. But you have to be super-good to make big money.

RACHEL: My coach and my surfing mates all reckon I've got the talent to make it. The only one who thinks I can't is my own mother! Brilliant!

She storms off towards her room.

PENNY: You dinner's in the oven!

RACHEL: I got a hamburger on the way home.

PENNY: So what's that cost you? Six dollars? Eight with chips? Add that to the steak that's going to waste in the oven and that adds up to money! My money!

RACHEL: God you're a scrooge. Money. Always money.

PENNY: Do you know what it cost me to have a new differential put in your car?

RACHEL: You should have bought me a newer model.

PENNY: I can't believe you sometimes. That repair cost me nearly two thousand dollars. Wiped out most of my reserve savings.

RACHEL: I didn't force you to buy the bloody car.

PENNY: It was either that or kill you, because you never bloody let up about having to have one.

RACHEL: The best waves are twenty K down the coast.

PENNY: On the next census form I'll enter our religion as wave bloody worship. Why don't you get your damned father to pay some of your expenses.

RACHEL: Because—

PENNY: Because he's a bloody no-hoper.

RACHEL: He has psychological issues.

PENNY: Yeah, acute fear of work.

RACHEL: He's still a nice person.

PENNY: Unlike me.

RACHEL *heads towards her room.*

Give me your phone.

RACHEL: No.

PENNY: If you take it to your room, you'll be messaging friends all the rest of the evening and you won't do a jot of work.

RACHEL: Some parents trust their daughters.

PENNY: The ones with daughters they can trust. Phone! And whatever homework you've been set, do it!

RACHEL: Thank God I go to Dad on the weekends.

PENNY: And his lovely new teen queen. Dimity.

RACHEL: She's nice to him. And me.

PENNY: She doesn't have to try and knock some sense into you.

RACHEL: When I get my first world championship you won't even get an invite to the party.

PENNY: You win a world championship and I'll sing Madonna's 'Sorry' on TikTok every day for a year, but in the meantime do your bloody homework and at least give yourself a chance at getting into uni.

RACHEL: [*angrily*] How many times do I have to tell you! I don't want to go to bloody uni. Why the fuck are you so obsessed about it!

PENNY: Because I don't want you to end up like me! A total shit job with a total shit boss, and yes, worrying about every bloody cent I spend. You have no idea what it's like.

RACHEL: I've heard it often enough.

PENNY: [*exploding*] You haven't heard the half of it!

RACHEL: What part haven't I heard!

PENNY: Lots!

RACHEL: Like what!

PENNY: Like, during the global recession I was cut back to two days a week and you were only a tot and your useless father had walked out and was out of work in any case. It was hell! They cut off electricity because I couldn't pay the bills and I had to use an Esky to keep your food from rotting and light the bloody place with candles. And beg friends for enough hand-me-downs and blankets to keep you warm through winter. And I had to drive without a licence or insurance and was as scared as hell I'd get pulled over. Why am I obsessing about you getting qualified? Because I'm trying to get it through your thick skull that life without money isn't life, it's just bloody day-to-day grinding existence and that's not what I want for you! It was only three or so years ago I finally got back on full time. I want you qualified so you don't ever have to live the shit life I've led!

RACHEL *is taken aback by her mother's outburst, even more so when* PENNY *sinks down into a chair with tears forming in her eyes.*

I want you to have a real life. A life with options.

She looks up at RACHEL.

You know what I wanted to be?

RACHEL: What?

PENNY: A doctor. My favourite TV show was *House MD*, about this genius doctor who solved difficult cases and saved people. I had this fantasy that I'd be like him and save people. And feel great. I mean it was stupid. But being a doctor wasn't. I was doing really well at all the subjects I needed and I was on track to get the marks I needed and I had a teacher who believed and found out all the scholarships I could apply for, and maybe I could've even still somehow managed if my mum and dad hadn't been such total pricks when they found out I was pregnant. If Gran hadn't taken me in I don't know what the hell I would've done.

RACHEL: What's the message? Having me has ruined your life?

PENNY: No!

RACHEL: You didn't have to have me.

PENNY: Yes I did. Bloody hell I did. There was no way I wasn't going to have you.

RACHEL: Why?

PENNY: Because I couldn't bloody bear the thought of never knowing what you would have been like.

RACHEL: Well now you know and wish you didn't.

PENNY: You were the best little kid.

RACHEL: And now I'm a horror?

PENNY *sighs.*

PENNY: Maybe you can make it as a surfer. But for me it's a big maybe. Can you understand that? You might think I don't give a shit about you but you are very very wrong. You're all I really care about. Is it a crime to want you to have a much better life than I have? And I'm not just talking about money! I want you to be able to do something you love doing. That must be the best thing that can ever happen to anyone.

RACHEL *gets up and moves across to her mother and hugs her briefly then moves off. Then turns.*

RACHEL: Mum, how many million times do I have to tell you. I've already found the thing I love doing.

She disappears in the direction of her room. PENNY *watches her go and sighs.*

In her living room next evening, PENNY *hears the front doorbell ring. She goes and opens the door.* GRACE *stands there.*

PENNY: Can I help you?

GRACE: I rang before. I'm Grace Delahunty, Alex Whittle's PA. She wants to meet you.

PENNY: The only time I want to lay eyes on your boss is in a car driving out of town. Preferably a hearse.

GRACE: Can I come in. Please?

PENNY *leads her in.*

PENNY: I won't change my mind.

GRACE: Please just hear me out.

PENNY *indicates a sofa.* GRACE *sits and* PENNY *sits in a chair opposite. There's a silence.*

Penny, I've worked for Alex for nearly eighteen years.

PENNY: Okay.

GRACE: I've done my very best to be diligent and efficient and I think that I've served her as well as any human could.

PENNY: You still are.

GRACE: As a matter of fact I'm not. Not any longer. I'm used to her treating me appallingly. She does it to everyone. It's part of the territory. But this morning was the tipping point. This morning she gave me a warning that I'd better improve because I had the temerity to cancel a meeting she told me to cancel and find her a room that didn't live up to her grandiose expectations.

PENNY: Not nice, but I would've thought you'd had worse.

GRACE: I have, much worse believe me.

PENNY: Why did you work for her for so long?

GRACE: She pays top dollar. And that's enabled me to save enough for a quite reasonable retirement. But what was different this morning was the warning. She forgot I know how she operates. Alex gives no warnings. A warning means you're finished. The end. Kaput. The minute I left the room she would have been on the phone to her personnel manager instructing him to find my replacement.

PENNY: What exactly am I hearing here?

GRACE: There's a story I rather like. This guy is watering his garden and sees his next door neighbour and says to her 'I like your husband's new Mercedes,' and she says 'Would you like to buy it?' 'How much?' he says. 'Twenty-five dollars,' she says. 'Really?' he says? 'Yes,' she says. 'He told me he was in New York on business but I found out he's got a mistress there. So what he's doing to her over there, I'm doing to him back here.'

PENNY: Would we possibly be talking revenge?

GRACE: Have you ever felt that urge?

PENNY: Often. But I've never been in a position to make it happen.

GRACE: Well I am. And I'm really enjoying the thought.

PENNY: And I'm enjoying you enjoying the thought.

GRACE: I'd love to buy a little cottage here, but not if Alex succeeds in taking over this town.

PENNY: The golf club but not exactly the town.

GRACE: Oh there's lot's lot more than the golf club.

PENNY *stares at her.*

PENNY: What?

GRACE: Much more. The golf club is just a lure to attract wealth and sell her adjoining luxury apartments.

PENNY: What's the rest of her plan?

GRACE: Turn Wallis Heads into our prime coastal wealth destination. She's secretly bought a heap of prime real estate cheap plus three prime commercial sites and wants council permission to build a luxury hotel and two multi-storey luxury apartment blocks on them.

PENNY: The council has a four-storey limit on commercial development.

GRACE: It's only a recommendation, and the council is totally in her pocket.

PENNY: This is unbelievable!

GRACE: She's got deposits on most of the beachfront commercial as well. She'll lease it all out to high-end fashion boutiques and fine-dining restaurants and keep the freehold on the best of them. She's done her homework. Byron Bay and Noosa have been loved to death. The smart IT kids who can work anywhere and high-net-worth retirees are looking for a new lifestyle nirvana. And high-spend tourists will love it. You can kiss your laid-back village lifestyle goodbye. In five years' time there'll be so much gold jewellery on your main street you'll be hospitalising people blinded by the dazzle.

PENNY: My God, this is awful!

GRACE: Barring a miracle it'll all happen.

PENNY: She's bought secretly? How can you buy secretly?

GRACE: When you've got an army of lawyers and accountants, easily. You'd have to trace back through ten or more shell companies located in the world's tax havens to get to her.

PENNY: Could we trace it back to her?

GRACE: Not unless you can afford a team of top forensic accountants. But not to worry. I'll photocopy the ownership trail for you.

PENNY: Won't that put you at risk?

GRACE: She'll assume someone on council leaked it.

PENNY: Alex isn't exactly loved around town already. This could turn things right around.

GRACE: Be warned. Her PR gurus have worked out a way to soften her image.

PENNY: How?

GRACE: She's setting up a charitable foundation.

PENNY: To do what?

GRACE: Scholarships to talented local kids whose parents are struggling.

PENNY: Surely no-one'll fall for that.

GRACE: People are easily manipulated by a bit of media razzle-dazzle. Berlusconi, Trump, Bolsonaro, Boris Johnson, Scott Morrison? A few photos of Alex smiling, her arms around the kids she's helping and half the population will sigh and say, 'How lovely.'

PENNY *shakes her head in disgust.*

So I can tell her you don't want to meet her?

PENNY: I'd rather have a candlelight dinner with Mark Latham.

GRACE: Good for you. She only wants to do it so she can intimidate you.

PENNY: She's not going to have the chance.

Beat.

Grace, thanks. I've got some real ammunition now.

GRACE: Don't get your hopes up too high. Nobody's got the better of her yet.

GRACE *sighs.*

Now to earn my last paycheque, I have to go and find some kid with exceptional talent.

The next day, ALEX *is standing in the middle of her hotel suite reading a list that* GRACE *has given her.*

ALEX: This is it? Five names?

GRACE: This was the consensus about the best of the best from the schools and the sporting clubs and music and drama groups. There are more at a lower level you can take later on.

ALEX: [*reading*] Nicole McSweeny. Sixteen, actor.

GRACE: Very good apparently. She's been in a lot of local productions and they think she's a future star.

ALEX: Why aren't we allowed to say 'actress' any more? I hate that.

GRACE: She's apparently very good.

ALEX: Actress—no way. Fail rate too high. We want someone with a real chance of making it big and being called Nicole isn't enough to get her there.

GRACE: Young Simone McNeil is doing amazingly well in her ballet classes.

GRACE *shows her a photo.*

ALEX: Grace, she's only eleven! She'll probably look like a plum pudding by the time she's eighteen.

[*Reading*] Rachel Poulter. Seventeen. Top surfing talent. Surfer? Are you joking? There are more promising young surfers in this beach-crazed country than there are lefties in the ABC. Ah. Here we are. Norman Seaton, fifteen. Exceptional tennis talent. Ranked second in the state in his age group. This guy sounds the real deal.

GRACE: Here's his photo.

ALEX: [*looking*] Ah, cute kid. Melt your heart. He'll photograph brilliantly. Predicted to make the nation's top-five players. This is our guy … We'll have him in whites and I'll wear red or green—anything goes with white doesn't it. What do you think, Grace? Red or green?

GRACE: I'd go green. Soothing colour.

ALEX: The fuck with soothing? Why soothing? We're trying to grab attention.

GRACE: Sorry. Red.

ALEX *looks at the photo again and nods her head in approval. She looks at the list again and frowns.*

ALEX: Poulter. Rachel Poulter? That troublemaker? Mrs Crocs-on-Camera? The one who won't ever deign to meet me? She's called Poulter? Isn't she?

GRACE: Penny Poulter. Yes.

ALEX: Is that her daughter maybe?

GRACE: I don't know.

ALEX: Then find out. Quickly.

A few days later, GRACE *ushers* RACHEL *into* ALEX*'s hotel suite.* ALEX *mightn't think it's grand but as she looks around the anteroom it's obvious that* RACHEL *does.* ALEX *is at her most charming and motherly as she smiles at* RACHEL. GRACE *retreats.*

Rachel! How lovely to see you. And congratulations.

RACHEL: [*a little overwhelmed*] Thanks.

ALEX: I suppose you're wondering what this is all going to mean for you?

RACHEL: Yeah. Yes.

ALEX: Well the new is all good. All good. Where do you want your life to go from here, Rachel? What's your dream?

RACHEL: Ah …

ALEX: Come on. Don't hold back.

RACHEL: It might seem a bit … big-headed, but …

ALEX: Rachel, that's what's wrong with this country. We limit our aspirations. Being big-headed isn't a sin. It's a sign that deep down you want to be the very best version of yourself you can possibly be. What's your dream?

RACHEL: I want to be world champion.

ALEX: Then don't be scared to say it. In fact hold your head high and shout it! 'I want to be world champion.' And I'll promise you something. My foundation will do everything possible to help you get there.

RACHEL *gives a big sigh of relief.*

RACHEL: This is so …

ALEX: So what?

RACHEL: Amazing. So different.

ALEX: From what?

RACHEL: From my mother.

ALEX: How so?

RACHEL: All I get from her is negativity.

ALEX: Surely she must realise how talented you are?

RACHEL: No way.

ALEX: Second in the state?

RACHEL: Doesn't mean a thing. Pass your exams, go to university, same old same old …

ALEX: I went to university, Rachel, and after the first year I realised it wasn't teaching me anything even halfway useful for the future I wanted for myself and I left. And I haven't done so badly.

RACHEL: [*with tears in her eyes*] It's just such a … It's just so good to have someone … believe in you.

ALEX *goes across and puts an arm around her shoulder.*

ALEX: I had parents who didn't believe in me too. I was the kid in my family my parents wished they'd never had. The ugly one, the dumb one, the clutzy one, the one without any social graces. The one my father thought was destined for failure and who told me so often. The good thing about your parents not believing in you is anger. It fuels you. It gives you the energy to prove them wrong. Use that anger.

RACHEL: I'm going to.

ALEX: The best moment in my life was when my father went bankrupt. I bought him a luxury apartment, gave him an allowance and told him never to contact me again.

RACHEL: Wow. I don't hate Mum that much.

ALEX: If she doesn't believe in you, then maybe you should. To be lucky enough to have such a talented daughter and to not acknowledge it? That's a massive negative in my book.

RACHEL: Yeah, and mine.

ALEX: The foundation is going to do everything possible to help you prove her wrong.

RACHEL *lowers her head to hide the tears and nods her head vigorously.*

RACHEL: Sorry about what my mum said about you.

ALEX: To tell you the truth when your name came up I asked myself if I really wanted to help the daughter of the woman who had just trashed me.

RACHEL: Don't blame you.

ALEX: I crossed you off the list and decided to go with number two. Some young tennis kid.

RACHEL: Norm Seaton. Yeah he's pretty good.

ALEX: But finally I couldn't do it. People call me tough and ruthless and that may be true but I also have integrity. It's lost me quite a bit of money over my lifetime but at least I can sleep at night.

RACHEL: I'm really really grateful.

ALEX: My assistant and I put our thinking caps on about where you should go from here and I think we've come up with a pretty exciting possibility.

ALEX *smiles warmly at her.* RACHEL *leans forward in anticipation.*

I've got a feeling you're going to like this.

A little while later, PENNY *is in the kitchen when* RACHEL *bursts in, excited. She runs over and hugs her mother.*

PENNY: You get an A in Ancient History?

RACHEL: Ancient History is ancient history. You want me to go to university?

PENNY: Yes. Of course.

RACHEL: Well your dreams have just come true.

PENNY: What are you talking about? Your final exams are months away.

RACHEL: I've got a scholarship.

PENNY: To where?

RACHEL: University of California San Diego.

PENNY: What?

RACHEL: It was just confirmed today. All I've got to do is get enough credits to get my QCE and I'm in.

PENNY: Hang on. What are we talking about here? An American university?

RACHEL: University of California San Diego. Named by *Forbes* magazine as the fourteenth best university in the US.

PENNY: What kind of scholarship?

RACHEL: A surf scholarship. They've got a top-ranking college surf team.

PENNY: They've got a degree in surfing?

RACHEL: Marine Biology. They want a great surf team.

PENNY: You want to do Marine Biology?

RACHEL: Biology is the only subject I like at school.

PENNY: The way you're going at the moment you won't get enough credits to get your QCE?

RACHEL: I'm motivated now. I'll knock it out of the ball park.

PENNY: This is …

RACHEL: Is what? You're not happy for me?

PENNY: No, it's great. It's just … daughter off to California. It's a shock.

RACHEL: Everything's paid. Accommodation on campus. Food. An allowance. A generous allowance.

PENNY: The school applied on your behalf?

RACHEL: No. The foundation. They're paying the expenses not covered by the scholarship.

PENNY: Foundation?

RACHEL: Alex Whittle. Okay, I know what you think of her and she isn't exactly a fan of yours either but she still named me as the first scholarship winner.

PENNY *stares at her, speechless.*

You're not even going to congratulate me?

PENNY: Do you know why Alex Whittle's here?

RACHEL: Yeah, you told me. She's making a golf course. Okay.

PENNY: That land was promised for social housing! And that's just the start of what she's doing!

RACHEL: What's she doing?

PENNY: She's buying up half the town to turn it into what she calls a 'high-end wealth destination'.

RACHEL: This place could do with a makeover.

PENNY: High-rise towers on the beachfront?

RACHEL: It'd make it exciting like the Gold Coast.

PENNY: You'd like us to become like the Gold Coast?

RACHEL: Mum, Wallis Heads is tired. It's old-world. Our main street shops look like they're out of a doco on the gold rush days.

PENNY: I love this town the way it is. I thought you did too.

RACHEL: Face it, Mum, it's in a bloody time warp. If Alex's got the money to make it exciting, then great.

PENNY: Huge towers casting a shadow over the beach from one-thirty. Like the Gold Coast?

RACHEL: Why do you keep knocking the Gold Coast? It's a hell of a lot more lively than this place.

PENNY: Rachel, she's planning to turn this town into a chic enclave for the super-wealthy. We'll most probably be evicted so some hedge-fund manager can knock this house down and build a glass-and-concrete palace.

RACHEL: You can't stop progress.

PENNY: Well I'm going to bloody well try! That kind of progress in any case.

RACHEL: How?

PENNY: Try and get rid of this deadbeat council. I get how you feel but she's using you. My daughter—the first kid to be helped by her foundation?

RACHEL: What are you saying? I only got this offer so she could embarrass you?

PENNY: More than possible.

RACHEL: You really really don't think I amount to anything do you?

PENNY: If I was Alex and I wanted to dream up the best way to make me look like a goose, this would be it.

RACHEL: She sent my surfing clips off to UCSD. And they jumped at the chance to have me in their competition surf team. And they're rated number one in the US. There's still no chance in your mind that I might have got this on my merits.

PENNY: [*sobered*] Really?

RACHEL: Yes really?

PENNY: Look the offer might be real, but …

RACHEL: The offer is real! Mum, this is the chance of a lifetime. This is the full booyaa for me!

PENNY: Booyaa?

RACHEL: The ultimate. The dream. There's no way I'm going to turn it down because you want to keep this the town that time forgot.

She storms off, slamming the door behind her. Then re-emerges still angry.

You're wrong about Alex. She's a much better person than you think.

PENNY: Really? Tell me how?

RACHEL: When she realised I was your daughter she was going to pick someone else. But she couldn't bring herself to penalise me because of who my mother was. Is that someone who's a monster?

RACHEL *turns around and goes back into her room, slamming the door behind her.*

Next day, GRACE *is waiting in a café. She starts to text a message when* PENNY *hurries in and sits down.*

PENNY: Sorry.

GRACE: That's fine. I haven't been here long. You've heard? About Rachel.

PENNY: And California. When I put it to her that it might be Alex making me look like a goose, she had the mother of tantrums.

GRACE: I'm not sure I should tell you this then.

PENNY: Tell me what?

GRACE: If it gets to Rachel it could sour your relationship for ever.

PENNY: Rachel wasn't number-one pick?

GRACE: Not until Alex realised who she was. Alex had chosen some young tennis prodigy.

PENNY: Norman Seaton?

GRACE *nods.*

GRACE: Please don't let on that you know. Alex will know it had to come from me.

PENNY: Of course not.

GRACE: This is vintage Alex. Sorry.

PENNY: She's made herself Rachel's number-one all-time hero.

GRACE: It's no accident she's Australia's richest woman. Can I order you a coffee?

PENNY *nods.*

PENNY: And a packet of antidepressants.

Next day, ALEX *taps a number into her iPhone in her hotel suite.*

ALEX: Grace!

She frowns impatiently.

Grace!

GRACE: [*voice only*] Yes, Alex.

ALEX: Send in Penny Poulter.

GRACE: [*voice only*] She just left. She said she wasn't waiting around any longer.

ALEX: Well, precious old her.

GRACE: [*voice only*] She's still waiting for the lift. I can see her.

ALEX: Get her.

ALEX *preens herself in front of a mirror with a wry smile on her face, which she wipes off when* PENNY *enters.*

Please take a seat.

PENNY *nods and sits on a two-person settee across from* ALEX*'s chair.* ALEX *sits, taking her time.* GRACE *stays, noting the conversation in her notebook.*

You wanted to see me?

PENNY: You're surprised?

ALEX: Not really. I thought you might want to thank me for the help I'm giving your daughter?

PENNY: It's a low act.

ALEX: Low act? Refusing to penalise your highly talented daughter just because her mother is trying her best to make my life as difficult as possible. I think the town will find that admirable.

PENNY: A surf scholarship?

ALEX: Yes, they offer three a year. Of course it's only five thousand dollars but the foundation will pick up all the other expenses.

PENNY: For the full three years of the degree?

ALEX: For the first year. After that it's up to you.

PENNY: Do you know how much US tuition costs?

ALEX: We'll have given her a very good start. There are other talented kids we have to help.

PENNY: Brilliant. Win over the town, make me the town doofus, then leave me without the a hope in hell of helping her finish her course.

ALEX: We're giving her a flying start.

PENNY: Yeah, and then leaving her high and dry.

ALEX: If she's any good she'll be a circuit pro by then.

PENNY: And if she isn't, you don't give a damn.

PENNY, *disgusted, gets up to walk out.*

ALEX: How long have you been living here, Penny?

PENNY *turns back.*

PENNY: Almost twenty years.

ALEX: Enjoying one of the most beautiful places on earth with an almost perfect climate and paying a very modest rent. Haven't you been lucky.

PENNY: Not for much longer if you have your way. It'll be the land of bling, stretched skin and labradoodles.

ALEX: What makes think you're entitled to hang on to your blessed lifestyle forever if more successful people than you are willing to pay more for it?

PENNY: Money's the whole deal, yeah?

ALEX: Nobody's going to hand you the title deeds to property because you've got a sweet personality. Sorry, honey, but money is always going to decide who gets what, which means that it's highly likely things are going to go my way.

PENNY: Maybe.

ALEX: Maybe?

PENNY: Maybe it's going to be a bit tougher than you think.

ALEX: [*alert*] In what way?

PENNY: The town's about to learn stuff.

ALEX: [*sharply*] What stuff?

PENNY: Like, er … two luxury tower blocks on the beach? A luxury hotel? Way over the height limits. And deposits all over the joint on our best residential and commercial land.

ALEX: [*tense*] Where did you hear that?

PENNY: A little bird told me.

ALEX: [*angrily*] That bird is about to get its arse sued for breach of confidentiality, so I hope it can fly fast.

PENNY: [*turning to leave*] Shouldn't be too hard to catch. I think it's nesting somewhere in the council chambers.

ALEX*'s eyes narrow.*

ALEX: Penny, people who try and stand in my way always end up bruised.

PENNY: I'm pre-bruised, Alex. Pretty much immune by now.

ALEX: We'll see.

PENNY: Ditto for you, princess. When people find out what you're planning you might find there's more opposition than you bloody well think. Might be an idea to get those mirrors-on-sticks to check under your car.

ALEX: Are you threatening violence?

PENNY: Not me. I'm full on virtuous poverty. It's those mad Greenies who want to take us back to the Stone Age. They're the worry.

PENNY *goes out the door.* ALEX *is furious. She turns to* GRACE.

ALEX: Did you get that down? That blatant threat?

GRACE: Sorry, Alex. I thought you wanted all this off-record.

ALEX: You heard what she said though?

GRACE: Sorry, no. I nodded off. I was up late pressing all your other suits just in case.

ALEX *stares at* GRACE *and shakes her head in disbelief.*

Later that day, ALEX *has summoned* ALAN *and* BRIAN *to her suite. She's still furious.*

ALEX: Someone in the council leaked!

ALAN: They wouldn't. It wouldn't be in any of our interests. We all want this to happen.

ALEX: Well some shit-for-brains numbchuck doesn't! And it has to have been one of your colleagues. Brian, when our local Erin Brockovitch spreads the details of my plan it's going to be huge news. How you cover it is going to make a big difference. No big front-page sensationalism, please.

BRIAN: Alex, I own the paper, I edit the paper. I decide how my news is going to be treated.

ALEX: Brian, don't get precious. My accountants tell me you're running at a loss because you can't get enough advertising.

BRIAN: We're beefing up our advertising sales team.

ALEX: From one to one more part time? That's not going to save you. What will save you is advertising from greatly increased commercial activity.

BRIAN: I can't let that influence the way I treat news.

ALEX: Brian, you're very endearing. Quite *To Catch a Mockingbird* Gregory Peck-ish, but please get real. At the moment *The Wallis Heads Advocate* would sell for less than my old Sony Walkman. If you help this town achieve its potential, then in four to five years' time you could sell it for a fortune and retire in style.

BRIAN: I won't overplay or underplay. But I won't be told how to treat this issue or any issue in the future.

ALAN: For Christ's sake, Brian, take off your crusader's cape! The word is that the Greenies are trying to recruit Penny Poulter to run for mayor.

ALEX: She's a shelf-stacker!!

ALAN: She is smart and tenacious and people trust her and she knows everyone.

ALEX: We'll outspend them ten to one. Twenty to one.

ALAN: There are a lot of tree-huggers in town who'll vote for them.

ALEX: No-one's going to vote in a pack of financially illiterate lunatics.

ALAN: The only cash flow they've ever handled came over a Centrelink counter.

ALEX: Brian, you're surely not going to treat them as serious contenders?

BRIAN: Their inexperience does weigh against them. I'll take that into account.

ALEX: Brian, stop being so fuckwittedly even-handed. This town stays as it is and your paper is dead in the water.

BRIAN: I can't let my commercial interests influence my editorial content.

ALEX: Murdoch's been doing it for fifty years and he's made seventy billion.

ALAN: For God's sake, get off your moral high horse!

BRIAN *gets up to leave.*

BRIAN: I won't sit here and be told what to do by anyone!

ALEX: I'm not telling you what to do. But if you don't you're roadkill.

BRIAN *grunts angrily as he leaves.*

ALAN: He's really pissed off. If we lose him we could be in big trouble.

ALEX: I've never lost a fight yet and I've faced far more formidable opponents than Penny Poulter and her deep-green dickheads!

ALAN: People like her.

ALEX: Nobody's a saint. There has to be something she's done we can leak to social media. An affair with a married man?

ALAN: Do we need to go down that path?

ALEX: We need to go down any path that will get her out of the picture. Does your wife belong to a book group?

ALAN: Yes but—

ALEX: Most efficient gossip machines on the planet. Ask her if she's heard anything. I've had my people trolling through social media but so far nothing more than her drinking 'sex on the beach' cocktails on Friday nights with her girlfriends. Ask your wife.

That afternoon, ALEX *has called* GRACE *into the office.*

Somebody leaked my development plans and they're about to be printed in the local rag.

GRACE: Really?

ALEX: Council were told they were strictly confidential.

GRACE: Someone must have leaked.

ALEX: Yes, but why is what puzzles me. It could only be someone on the council and they all want this to happen.

GRACE: It doesn't seem to make sense, but then, human emotions often don't.

ALEX: Spare me your profundity, Grace. Just get the launch of my foundation organised. Write a speech for Rachel to read. We want the press to get exactly the right message. And get her in here. We need to check if her mum, Little Betsy Bucolic, is poisoning the well.

Later that afternoon, ALEX *talks to* RACHEL, *sitting opposite her and doing a good imitation of a kindly old aunt.*

So how are things with your mother?

RACHEL: What do you think?

ALEX: I'd hoped that wouldn't be the case.

RACHEL: Greatest opportunity in my life and she's still totally negative.

ALEX: It's apparently a top university.

RACHEL: I checked out the website. It's kickass. Savage.

ALEX: Which I presume means it's good?

RACHEL: Awesome.

ALEX *nods in acknowledgement.*

ALEX: I'm about to announce my foundation to the town and I'd like you to be there with me.

RACHEL: Sure. Happy to.

ALEX: Your mother won't be pleased.

RACHEL: My mother can go to hell. She's never believed in me.

ALEX: So sad.

RACHEL: Never once.

ALEX: She knows you'll be doing a degree in Marine Biology? I just don't get it.

RACHEL: Don't try. I've given up.

ALEX: Has she told you she's planning to stand for mayor?

RACHEL: [*startled*] No. But that would be typical. Never tells me anything.

ALEX: Really?

RACHEL: I find out eventually.

ALEX: Not good when a parent hides things.

RACHEL: Sometimes for good reason.

ALEX: Really.

RACHEL: She's no saint I can tell you.

ALEX: What's she done?

RACHEL: Things she wouldn't like known, I can tell you.

ALEX: Rachel, if your mother and her cronies do win the election then you realise they'll block everything I want to do.

RACHEL: The foundation?

ALEX: All over, red rover.

RACHEL: No California.

ALEX: Sorry.

RACHEL: Shit!

ALEX: Rachel, I'd never try and ask you to do something you wouldn't want to do, but if your mother has done something she feels she has to hide, then couldn't this be something the voters should know? Aren't they entitled to know exactly who they're electing?

RACHEL: [*worried*] You wouldn't ever say where it came from?

ALEX: Of course not.

RACHEL *hesitates.*

RACHEL: No. Can't.

RACHEL *looks away.*

ALEX: Your whole future could be at stake here.

RACHEL *hesitates again.*

RACHEL: She … No, sorry. I can't.

A little later, when RACHEL *has gone,* ALEX *calls* GRACE *in.*

ALEX: Grace, what was the name of those private investigators we used to ferret out the dirt on Robbie Macklin?

[*Off* GRACE*'s frown*] Rachel let slip that her mother has something murky back there in her past.

GRACE: Do you really want to go down that path?

ALEX: [*angriy*] Do you know how much money's to be made if this thing goes ahead?

GRACE: A lot.

ALEX: Huge, but it's still a risk, and Penny standing for mayor is starting to worry me. Get me their number. They're really good.

Later that evening, RACHEL *is in her room doing her homework.* PENNY *comes in holding a copy of the Wallis Heads newspaper.*

RACHEL: [*holding up her homework for her mother to see*] Ancient History. Hannibal. Happy?

PENNY: [*pointing at the headlines*] Alex is about to announce her foundation.

RACHEL: Yeah.

PENNY: So are you going to be part of it?

RACHEL: Yeah.

PENNY: And you'll thank her?

RACHEL: Mum, this is like a dream come true for me.

PENNY: Yeah.

RACHEL: But what would you care? As far as you're concerned it's all about you.

PENNY: No. It's all about this town.

RACHEL: It's all about what you want this town to be. You didn't even bother to tell me you were standing as mayor.

PENNY: I only finally decided yesterday.

RACHEL: [*suddenly passionate*] If your side wins it's the end of the foundation. I never get to join the best young surf team in the world.

PENNY: Darling, this is your dream. I get that, but maybe I'm fighting about a bigger issue.

RACHEL: [*flaring*] Everything's a bigger issue than me isn't it? Why do you want this shitty little town to keep looking like a retrowreck!

PENNY: Shitty little town? Drive up to the headland and look down on it.

RACHEL: What do you want me to do? Knock back the scholarship? And the foundation money.

Beat.

Okay. It's embarrassing for you. I get that. But it's brilliant for me.

PENNY *goes to walk away.*

Can't you at least acknowledge that Alex is being incredibly generous?!

This is too much for PENNY. *She turns back.*

PENNY: Did Alex tell you that she's only funding the first year of your course?

RACHEL: [*staring at her*] No.

PENNY: Do you know how much tuition costs a year? Over forty thousand US dollars. There's no way I could fund you for the next two.

RACHEL: Okay, not cool, but even one year would be great. I'll be amongst the best. I'd learn so much. I'd have a real chance of going pro. But of course you'd never believe that, would you?

PENNY: I rang UCSB.

RACHEL: Why? You didn't think it's all kosher?

PENNY: I had my doubts. I spoke to the head surfing coach and they loved what they saw on your clips. They thought you were great. Sorry.

RACHEL: An apology?

PENNY: [*flaring*] Yes! I'm saying sorry!

RACHEL: What you really should say sorry about is laying it on me that I only got this gig because Alex wanted to embarrass you!

This gets under PENNY*'s skin and finally tips the balance.*

PENNY: You weren't the first choice. When Alex realised who you were, that's when you became the first choice.

RACHEL *stares at her.*

RACHEL: Jesus, Mum. You'll try anything.

PENNY: Sorry but it's true.

RACHEL: How would you know that? Alex phones and tells you she's fucked you over?

PENNY: She'd settled on young Norm Seaton.

RACHEL: [*staring at her*] You're making this up.

PENNY: I wasn't ever going to tell you but … she's such a liar!

RACHEL: How do you know?

PENNY: I know.

RACHEL *looks stunned. Tears form in her eyes.* PENNY *goes across to put her arms around her.*

I'm sorry. I'm so so sorry.

RACHEL *pushes her away violently.*

RACHEL: Fuck off!

PENNY: Sorry. I'm really sorry.

RACHEL *turns on her eyes blazing.*

RACHEL: You know what? I don't give a shit! You get one great opportunity in your life and I've just got mine. I'm going to California! And I'm going to live at Dad's! He understands me one hell of a lot better than you! I don't give a shit how I got this chance, I'm grabbing it.

She runs out of the room, crying. RACHEL *sits down on the nearest chair and slumps.*

INTERVAL

A few days later, GRACE *waits for someone in a quiet corner of a bar. She's nursing a white wine. She looks at her watch. She's about to get up and go when* PENNY *appears.*

PENNY: So sorry I'm late. Strategy meeting with my election team.

GRACE: You're definitely standing for mayor.

PENNY: Yes. And we've got an impressive team of candidates challenging the pro-Alex mob.

GRACE: Ah.

PENNY: Why 'ah'?

GRACE: As you well know, my esteemed boss is a gutter fighter.

PENNY: I'm aware of that.

GRACE: She hired private eyes to ferret about in your past.

PENNY: They won't find anything.

GRACE: They did.

PENNY: What?

GRACE: You made money doing phone sex.

PENNY: Oh shit.

GRACE: It's true?

PENNY: It was true. I'd left my husband and he was out of work and paying no child support. I was cut to two days a week and Rachel was just a bub and the financial situation was desperate. And I didn't get back on full time for years so it kept being desperate. High school and she needed books, shoes, uniform, school excursions …

GRACE: Are you still doing it?

PENNY: No, not for three years now. As soon as I got a full-time gig I gave it up. But that won't make any difference, will it?

GRACE: No.

PENNY: Alex's going to release it?

GRACE: Not directly. It'll leak out on social media. Then the media will pick it up.

PENNY: Capital-city tabloids?

GRACE: For sure. It's sleaze gold for them. Mayoral candidate sells sex. Sorry, she's a monster.

PENNY: Would she still leak it if I quit the race for mayor?

GRACE: Knowing her, she might. Insurance in case you changed your mind.

Next morning, ALEX *waits in her anteroom. She walks to the window, looks out and then walks back and looks at her watch. She hits a number on her iPhone.*

ALEX: Grace, you can send her in.

PENNY *enters.*

Can I order coffee? Tea?

PENNY: I'm fine.

ALEX: I didn't expect a visit from you.

PENNY: Stop playing Little Miss Innocent. I know what you're about to do.

ALEX: I don't know what you're talking about?

PENNY: Yes you bloody well do.

ALEX: Not really.

PENNY: How low can you stoop, Alex?

ALEX: I have no idea what you're talking about.

PENNY: Of course you do. I just can't imagine any person except you using it.

ALEX: [*holding eye contact, intense*] In the sixties, Milton Friedman and the Chicago School of Economics changed the world. Profoundly. They told governments to cut the taxes of the wealthy and if they did, these Titans of finance would make big profits and reinvest those profits in new industries, create new jobs and we'd all grow richer faster. Which might have worked, except most of those Titans didn't reinvest and create new wealth. They stashed forty trillion dollars of profit into offshore tax havens. But I'm not one of those. The minute I make a profit with one venture I'm like a hawk up there circling, looking for my next. And because of that there are twenty-nine thousand families in apartments and houses I've built. Most of them ordinary Australians. I've also financed a massive offshore windfarm under construction that will generate half a gigawatt. And a solar farm in North Queensland that will power a quarter-of-a-million homes. None of this is out of the goodness of my heart but it still means I've done a hell of a lot more for the world than you ever will. So don't be so quick to turn me into the devil incarnate.

PENNY: What you're planning here is for the common good?

ALEX: No. This is for Australia's very wealthy. But it's also the biggest play I've made for quite some time. And it involves risk. Half-a-billion dollars' worth of risk. So. If I did know something embarrassing about you, do you do you really think I'd tie one arm behind my back to keep your little secret safe? Get real. For your sake and mine, quit the race.

PENNY: If I did, nothing would come out?

ALEX: There'd be no reason for it.

Beat.

So will you be pulling out?

PENNY *holds direct eye contact with* ALEX *for some time.*

PENNY: I was until a few seconds ago.

ALEX: Pull out. I'd rather not use it but I will if I have to.

PENNY: I know, but I can't turn this town over to the kind of people you want here. Greedy rich bastards who have never done anything for anyone but themselves in their whole lives. My net worth is near enough to zero, and most of the people I know here are the same. But it doesn't mean we're worthless. I've lost count of the small acts of kindness my friends have done for me over the years. I'm going to fight to keep my type of people here, not yours.

ALEX: My type of people always win. So good luck with that.

They hold eye contact for some seconds, then PENNY *turns and goes.*

Next evening, PENNY *is waiting for someone in the same bar. She's nursing a gin and tonic.* RACHEL *appears and sits down opposite her mother without saying a word.*

PENNY: Thanks for coming.

RACHEL: I'm not changing my mind.

PENNY: It's not about that. You do what you have to do.

RACHEL: So what's it about?

PENNY: This is … Alex's got some dirt on me and she's going to make sure people get to hear.

RACHEL: What?

PENNY: It's not great. I didn't ever want you to know.

RACHEL: Right.

PENNY: I just wanted you to be forewarned.
RACHEL: Right.
PENNY: Don't you want to hear what it is?
RACHEL: Oh. Er yeah.
PENNY: I could only get half-time work for years, I was getting no child support from your father, you were starting at school and …
RACHEL: And?
PENNY: I was a phone sex worker for years.
RACHEL: Oh.
PENNY: I wasn't all that good at it but I made enough to keep us afloat. Alex's bloodhounds found out.
RACHEL: Oh hell.
PENNY: Alex will spread it on social media. It will probably be picked up by the tabloids.
RACHEL: Tabloids? Sydney? Melbourne?
PENNY: 'Mayoral candidate does phone sex.'
RACHEL: Pull out of the race.
PENNY: I can't.
RACHEL: Mum, are you crazy? You're telling me you know what's going to happen and you're still going ahead.
PENNY: I can't back down. The people of this town deserve a choice!
RACHEL: I'm going to cop it too! Daughter of a sex worker?
PENNY: Yeah, I know.
RACHEL: But that's okay?
PENNY: No it's not. If I did pull out that'd be the reason.
RACHEL: But of course you won't pull out because you're so stubborn you teach bloody mules how to be stubborn.
PENNY: I couldn't face myself if I didn't fight!
RACHEL: You'll carry this for the rest of your life. You want that?
PENNY: Of course bloody not!
RACHEL: Then just admit she's won and step down, for Christ's sake!
PENNY: I can't.

Beat.

I hope—
RACHEL: What?
PENNY: You don't feel too—

RACHEL: What?

PENNY: Ashamed of me for …

RACHEL: What?

PENNY: Making money satisfying all kinds of grubby male fantasies.

RACHEL: Jesus, Mum. What do you think I am? Little Miss Prissy-Knickers? I'm seventeen.

PENNY: What's that mean?

RACHEL: You think any seventeen-year-old these days doesn't know something about grubby men's fantasies? I was listening to rap when I was twelve!

PENNY: Yes but you—

RACHEL: By the time I was fifteen I knew that men were an incurably grubby species and that you had to either live with that or become a nun. And nuns don't get to do much surfing.

PENNY: Yes but. …

RACHEL: Mum, don't do your headless-chook thing. It's okay. You were up against it. It was the only work you could get.

PENNY: I hated doing it. I felt really ashamed.

RACHEL: One day I'll tell you a few things I'm ashamed of when you're mature enough to cope with it.

PENNY: I didn't ever sleep with them.

RACHEL: It wouldn't particularly worry me if you had.

PENNY: It wouldn't?

RACHEL: Mum, it's called sex work. It's happened forever.

PENNY: If I do go ahead, there's going to be some bad stuff online, isn't there?

RACHEL: Hideous, so don't.

PENNY: I can't pull out now.

RACHEL: [*angrily*] Mum, you're not going to win in any case. Please just promise me that you'll call Alex tomorrow and tell her you've pulled out.

PENNY: I can't.

RACHEL: Then you're a total numbnut!

An angry RACHEL *turns on her heel and storms off.*

A few days later, ALEX *has* ALAN *in her office. He's sitting and she's pacing again and she's angry.*

ALEX: What are you telling me, Alan? The council's threatening to vote down my proposals?

ALAN: No. Not at this stage, no.

ALEX: Not at this stage?

ALAN: Thanks to Brian and his bloody journalistic 'integrity', everybody in the town knows about your development applications and it's a different ball game.

BRIAN: [*angrily*] I played it straight down the middle.

ALEX: Shadows over the beach by one-thirty? That helps us?

BRIAN: It's a fact that has to be reported.

ALAN: Not if you want us to win! Are you going to support our team editorially or not?

BRIAN: Yes I am! But the news I publish has to be objective.

ALAN: There's objective and too bloody objective.

BRIAN: No. There is only objective, objective.

ALEX: Brian if we are being objective, the objective fact is that objectively you are soon going to be bankrupt! Now stop being such a moralistic dickwit or that shelf-stacker will sink the whole bloody lot of us!

ALAN: Get the foundation launched. That'll help.

ALEX: It will, as long as Atticus Finch here doesn't relegate it to a paragraph on page bloody twenty.

BRIAN: I'll give it full coverage.

ALEX: With big colour photos. And make sure your photographer captures the money shot when my arm's around young Rachel, who with any luck will be tearing up.

ALAN: I'm sure the launch will steady the ship.

ALEX: If it doesn't I've still got a killer blow up my sleeve.

BRIAN: Killer blow?

ALAN: What?

ALEX: You don't need to know.

BRIAN: Perhaps I do.

ALEX: No you don't. In fact neither of you heard me even mention it. Just assume that Little Miss Righteous isn't going to be a worry.

ALAN: When does this thing we've never heard about happen?

ALEX: Let's get the foundation launched, then if my private polling shows that it still isn't enough then this will.

ALAN: You're sure?

ALEX: Alan, Mother Teresa wouldn't survive it.

ALAN *and* BRIAN *look at each other with frowns.*

An empty stage with a platform. ALAN, *as the mayor, makes an introduction. The media is all offstage nominally where the audience is.* GRACE *stands there at* ALEX*'s side.*

ALAN: Good afternoon and welcome to you, gentlemen and ladies of our local media. Contrary to some press stereotyping, Alex is in fact a generous and caring person who is planning to add far more to Wallis Heads than just bricks and mortar. I'm here today as your mayor to announce the first of her many initiatives. The Alex Whittle Creative Foundation, dedicated to identifying, financing and developing exceptional talent in our town. Here's Alex Whittle herself and the first lucky recipient of generous help from the foundation, brilliant young surfing prodigy, Rachel Poulter.

There's a gasp of surprise and buzz from the media as ALEX *and an embarrassed* RACHEL *come onstage.*

ALEX: Yes it might seem a bit odd that the first young talent I'm supporting is the daughter of a mayoral candidate who seems hellbent on torpedoing my plans to inject a large amount of much-needed development capital into this community. As I've admitted to Rachel, I was tempted to strike her name off the list of candidates, but I'm not that sort of person. Rachel was the best of the best and I couldn't penalise her because of her mother. Rachel has described this as an unbelievable dream come true, which makes what I'm doing with this foundation incredibly rewarding to me. But I'll let Rachel say a few words herself. Rachel?

RACHEL *steps forward hesitantly with the prepared speech in her hand. She looks down at it and puts it aside and looks intensely at the audience.*

RACHEL: When I was told I got this scholarship it was a dream come true. I thought, full marks to Alex. Choosing the daughter of her loudest opponent. Legend. But it turns out there was something else going on here. It turns out I only became the first choice when Alex found out I was Penny's daughter. But it was a great opportunity and I was still tempted. Big time. Then I found out a few more things that didn't sit easy with me. But let's be fair, Alex's scheme is a good one. Helping talented kids. Who could not like? So let's applaud the real winner, Alex's first first choice. Our very talented tennis prodigy, Normie Seaton.

ALEX: [*tersely*] What the fuck!

There is a loud babble of excitement and surprise from the media. ALEX *looks stunned and furious.* RACHEL *walks off the stage with* ALEX *staring after her.* GRACE, *standing beside* ALEX, *tries to wipe a big grin off her face when her boss turns towards her. A babble of questions are hurled at* ALEX *from the offstage press contingent.*

ALAN: [*lamely*] Congratulations, young Norman Seaton. As Shakespeare said, 'All's well that ends well.' Thanks for coming.

The lights snap off.

A little later in the evening, RACHEL *turns up in* PENNY*'s house.*

RACHEL: Hi Mum.

PENNY: Hi.

RACHEL: You heard?

PENNY: I heard.

She moves across to her daughter and hugs her.

Will you stay for dinner?

RACHEL *nods.*

RACHEL: Is it okay if I move back?

PENNY *nods.*

PENNY: I've been missing you like crazy.

RACHEL *goes to the door and brings in her suitcase, which she dumps in the doorway leading to her room.*

RACHEL: I can't take Dad's new girlfriend any longer. At least an airhead has air in her head. Dimity? Pure vacuum!

PENNY: That's the way your dad likes 'em. Used to give me underarm deodorant with aluminium in it 'cause he heard it lowered IQ.

Beat.

I know how much you wanted this. We'll get you there somehow. Crowd-fund.

RACHEL: No, here's fine. The California waves are shit compared with ours.

PENNY: Are you saying that to make me feel better.

RACHEL: No. I've got a real chance of winning the state title next year. The way UCSB reacted to my surf clips confirmed it.

PENNY: I've got a little bit stashed away and—

RACHEL: No, all my friends are here. My coach is one of the best in the world. I just got taken in by all the 'America is best' stuff we get hammered with all the time in the media.

PENNY: What you did today was … I cried for about ten minutes.

RACHEL: There's more to it, Mum.

PENNY *looks at her, frowning.*

I was the one who gave her the hint you were hiding something.

PENNY *stares at her daughter.*

I didn't say what, but she picked up on it. And no doubt got her bloodhounds onto it.

PENNY: How did you know?

RACHEL: The waves were shithouse one afternoon and I came home early.

PENNY: When I was doing it?

RACHEL: I actually thought it was a bit funny.

PENNY: Funny?

RACHEL: Not many kids have a mum who can have an orgasm shelling peas.

PENNY *holds out her arms and they hug. It's a hug of forgiveness.*

But for Christ's sake come to your senses and bloody well pull out of the race!

PENNY: I can't.

RACHEL: Mum, you've got as much chance of being elected as a Lesbian First Nations Green in Far North Queensland.

PENNY: I can't let Alex's stooges get back without a fight.

RACHEL: Mum, the tabloids will be bad enough but the online trolls—

PENNY: Yes, I know.

RACHEL: Okay. I give up. Live with it.

PENNY: And you live with the fact that if you're living back here you—

RACHEL: Get enough credits to pass my QCE? Don't worry. I'm doing a degree in Marine Biology here at USQ and I'm still going to win the world title, just to show you I can!

She gets up and carts her case offstage in the direction of her room. Her mother watches her go and shakes her head.

GRACE *has been summonsed by* ALEX, *who waits in her hotel suite anteroom later that evening.* GRACE *enters.*

GRACE: Yes, Alex.

ALEX: Something's been puzzling me, Grace.

GRACE: What's that?

ALEX: The leaks.
[*Off* GRACE*'s deadpan reaction*] So Penny gets to find out my precise development plans. A leak from council? Seems it has to be. But does it make sense. Why? All of them stand to benefit in a big way if my applications go through.

GRACE: Yes, it's puzzling.

ALEX: Yes it is. Then today. Rachel turns down something we all know she desperately wants and I've got egg, big time on my face.

GRACE: Yes, I was puzzled.

ALEX: How did she know that Norman Seaton was my first choice?

GRACE: A mystery.

ALEX: Tell me, Grace, who is the only person apart from myself that knew both my future plans for this town and the fact that we'd bumped Norman Seaton and chose Rachel? Take your time.

GRACE: Me.

ALEX: And that's how Penny knew I knew about the phone sex. You've been deliberately betraying me?

GRACE: Yes.

ALEX: After all I've done for you?

GRACE: Let me remind you what you've done for me, Alex. You've humiliated me at least once every single day I've worked for you. I've been called a fool, an idiot, and a moron. I've been told I'm incompetent, that hiring me was a mistake, that, your ten-year-old niece was smarter than I am, that someone forgot to pay my brain bill, that I must have fallen out of my family tree, that I was as bright as Hobart in winter, and quite a few more.

ALEX: Grace, don't be so bloody chi-chi.

GRACE: Alex, nobody has probably ever dared tell you this but you are a … fucking monster!

ALEX: And here's something you are … fired!

GRACE: I was fired over a week ago. You just weren't going to tell me until my replacement arrives.

ALEX: How did you know?

GRACE: She called me to ask what it was like to work for you. I told her, so now you'll have to find someone else.

ALEX: Get out of my sight.

GRACE: When you die, Alex, there'll be a lot of people at your funeral but not one of them will shed a single tear. When Penny Poulter dies there won't be as many but they'll weep buckets.

ALEX: Tears at a funeral? That's your test of success in life?

GRACE: It's a better one than the value of your estate.

GRACE *walks away, then turns back angrily.*

And if you have one decent bone in your body you won't let loose the media on Penny.

[*Off* ALEX*'s reaction*] But of course you will. The scorpion stings. It's in its nature.

This time she goes. ALEX *glares at her departing figure.*

On the large screen we see the gleeful media barrage play out. We get a taste of the horrors of the online vicious trolling on the social platforms such as Twitter and Facebook. Appalling messages such as 'Go away and die slut' 'Stick to cock sucking, bitch!' are briefly interspersed with smartarse headlines that shriek 'Phone Sex Mayor?' 'Penny offers electors a happy ending', 'Penny promises relief' 'Oh Come all Ye voters' And more moralistic stuff. 'Has she no shame?' 'Sex worker candidate—new electoral low'. Morning-show hosts make snide comments about how interesting it could be to ring the mayoral chambers if she wins.

PENNY *sits in a near catatonic trance in her living room.* RACHEL *comes home from school.*

RACHEL: Didn't go to work? Again?

PENNY: Couldn't face it.

RACHEL: I warned you!

PENNY: I didn't think it'd be this bad.

RACHEL: It's called a pile-on. Moralising pricks. Are you okay?

PENNY: No. Have you read any of today's trolls?

RACHEL: Don't!

PENNY: How am I supposed to cope with all that scorn and hate?

RACHEL: By remembering there are still plenty of good people in the world.

PENNY: Where have they gone?

RACHEL: They don't get a voice. The media gives its megaphone to the scumbags.

PENNY: Sure does.

RACHEL: They sell papers. They've stuffed up their own lives so they unload all their hate and envy on any target they can find.

PENNY: I'm sorry I didn't listen to you.

RACHEL *shakes her head ruefully.*

RACHEL: If ever there was a muley cadooley, it's you.

PENNY: I can't take it any more. I'm going to toss it in.

RACHEL: Don't you fucking dare! You've put us through all of this hell—it's not going to be for nothing!

PENNY: I'm not going to win.

RACHEL: I know! But for fuck's sake you're going to fight.

PENNY: Why?

RACHEL: Because there are good people out there.

PENNY: Who?

RACHEL: Even if you only get twenty percent that's still a lot of good people.

PENNY: You want to keep copping all this shit?

RACHEL: It's not as bad as I thought it'd be. The boys are their usual shitty snotty sneery smut-rag selves but the girls … a lot of them've been slut-shamed too.

PENNY: Slut-shamed? That's what I've been? Slut-shamed?

RACHEL: Big time. Mrs Mansfield—my psychology teacher—this just happened today—out of the blue—said to me that I had a very brave mother. She said everyone in town knows who's behind it and that a surprising amount would be on your side.

PENNY: Yeah?

RACHEL: I said to myself, shit yeah. And started to feel proud. Sure you're a mule-head but you've also got guts.

PENNY: Yeah, but—

RACHEL: Take the front foot, Mum. Keep fighting. Take her on. All this crap we've gone through has to be for something.

Some time later, PENNY *enters Brian's office.* BRIAN *looks up. There's a silence.*

BRIAN: So sorry.

PENNY: At least you didn't join the pile-on.

BRIAN: I was sickened by it.

PENNY: You know where it came from.

BRIAN: Yes.

PENNY: And you're still going to support her?

BRIAN: Unless there's more money pumped into this town, I'm facing bankruptcy.

PENNY: Brian, the community needs the paper. It's our lifeblood. If I'm elected the council will double its public-interest advertising.

BRIAN: Penny, you can't really think you're going to win. After this—

PENNY: I'd have a much better chance if you supported me.

BRIAN: I'd love to, but—

PENNY: The least you could bloody do is publish this.

She hands him a folder. He reads. Then looks at her.

Yeah, a challenge. A head-on bloody challenge.

ALEX *faces* BRIAN *and* ALAN. *She's got a copy of* The Wallis Heads Advocate *in her hands.*

ALEX: [*to* BRIAN] Why did you publish it? She's totally discredited. She's a joke. Why would I debate her?

BRIAN *indicates the paper.*

BRIAN: Since this came out I'm being inundated with emails and phone calls wanting it to happen.

ALAN: [*to* ALEX] Might be wise to do it. The mood is shifting out there.

ALEX: Fine. She wants it, she'll get it. I'll wipe the floor with her.

The debate is televised. PENNY *is on one side of the screen,* ALEX *on the other, with television reporter* JOEL *in the middle moderating. Onstage it's watched by* ALAN, RACHEL *and* BRIAN, *who are all in the studio audience.*

JOEL: Penny, perhaps we should start by addressing the elephant in the room. You still feel you're a viable future mayor given your—

PENNY: Given my lurid past? Yes I do, Joel. I did what I did out of sheer economic necessity. I didn't enjoy it but it served its purpose.

JOEL: A lot of media commentators are saying that you've ruled yourself out as a fit and proper person to occupy the high office of mayor?

PENNY: An opinion they're perfectly entitled to hold. But luckily we live in a democracy and I'll abide by the judgement of the electors.

JOEL: Alex. There is some talk around town that you could have been responsible for Penny's past becoming public knowledge.

ALEX: That's absolutely outrageous. Unlike some I play the game hard but I play it fair and honest.

JOEL: Do you have any thoughts on the moral issue. Is Penny a fit and proper person for high office?

ALEX: Frankly, if I were Penny I would have ruled myself out of the race long ago.

JOEL: Well, as Penny says it's up to the electors to decide. Penny, what's your vision of this town's future?

PENNY: I want Wallis Heads to remain a caring, inclusive community. Not just a picturesque backdrop for wealthy tourists to eat at ridiculously pricey restaurants and buy fashionwear and jewellery. And a place where wealthy residents build huge concrete-and-glass palaces that they occupy three weeks a year when they're not in Europe or on luxury cruises.

JOEL: And your vision, Alex?

ALEX: Not that ridiculous caricature of what is about to happen when I invest in a big way in this community. Yes, successful people will come here. And they will inject large amounts of money into the local economy and turn it into a thriving upmarket coastal gem that provides jobs, jobs and more jobs. Hotel management and reception, apprentice chefs, Uber drivers, waiters, local tour operators, surfing teachers, horse-riding instructors.

PENNY: Servants to the rich. Low-wage jobs whose workers won't be able to afford to rent in town and who will have to travel fifty Ks every day to and from work. If Alex's plans go ahead hundreds of renters who are already struggling to pay their rent and have been here for decades will be forced out.

ALEX: We live in a market economy. This is a beautiful town. More and more people are realising it and willing to pay good money to live here. To try and stop that is as useless as King Canute trying to hold back the tide.

JOEL: Is the tide unstoppable, Penny?

PENNY: This is a beautiful town and yes, people are going to come but if I'm elected they'll come on our terms. We'll restore the land earmarked for social housing and make a real effort to get it happening. We'll make the four-storey height recommendation mandatory, not just a suggestion. More public land will be gazetted as permanent National Park. We will ensure that Wallis Heads remains a place where ordinary Australians can still afford to live and where our natural beauty won't be destroyed.

JOEL: Okay, time to wrap this up. Alex?

ALEX: I'm prepared to risk hundreds of million of dollars to transform this town into one that'll be the envy of Australia. A town that people aspire to either visit or to live in. That's what I'll be creating. A place that, sure, not every one can afford, but one that everyone can aspire to, and without something to aspire to, what's the point of living?

JOEL: Penny?

PENNY: What's the point of living? For people like me it's to live in a caring community where money isn't everything. Which is hard and getting harder, because let's face it, this country has become the country of the great divide. On one side are Alex's people. On the other are mine. If Alex has her way, in ten years' time all my side of the divide will be able to do in Wallis Heads is press our noses against the glass wall of privilege and watch her lot do the dance of the no-limit American Express card. Elect me and I'll make sure that never happens.

JOEL: Well, that's it for this evening. Aspiration versus community. It's your choice. Thank you, Alex and Penny. You've given our voters a clear choice.

ALEX *is facing a worried* ALAN *and* BRIAN *just after the show in the studio.*

ALAN: [*gloomy*] Penny was impressive.

ALEX: And I wasn't?

ALAN: We're being deluged with angry texts and emails and voicemails. Your high-rise hotels in particular are getting a furious response.

ALEX: You back out now, Alan, and I'll have the best team of lawyers in Australia suing your council for the million-or-so dollars of planning money and legal advice spent on the assurance I'd get the permits to build.

ALAN: Calm down. We're still backing you, Alex. You just might need to increase your election spend.

ALEX: Jesus! I'm already spending money faster than a Saudi king's harem in Harrods.

ALAN: If you want this to happen we need more.

ALEX: [*to* BRIAN] I can still count on your support editorially?

ALAN: You're still with us?

BRIAN: No, sorry. I'm with Penny. I prefer her future to Alex's.

ALEX: You're happy to go bankrupt.

BRIAN: I'll take that risk.

ALEX: Get real. The town is never going to vote for Penny and her Green loonies. You've picked the losing side.

BRIAN: We'll see.

On the large television screen, we see a cheering room of supporters celebrating PENNY*'s victory.* PENNY *is in front of the microphone giving her thanks.*

PENNY: [*on screen*] I'd like to thank the people of Wallis Heads for putting their faith and trust in my team. I received a phone call from Alex Whittle a few minutes ago. I guess you could call it a congratulatory call except for the fact that she said I only won because everyone who voted for me had their head up their arse, but still.

The crowd laugh.

Okay, Alex is quitting here and turning her attention elsewhere but as I warned you our fight will never be over. There'll be other Alexes who'll want to do what she did. But I swear to you I will fight with all my strength and heart to make sure that they don't succeed.

A few days later, ALEX *faces* PENNY, *who has come to see her in her hotel anteroom. There are packed suitcases on the floor as she prepares to leave.*

ALEX: What do you want?

PENNY: Maybe an apology for the fact that I'll be sniggered at behind my back for the rest of my life, but of course that's never going to happen is it.

ALEX: I gave you the option to withdraw.

PENNY: And if I had you would've been starting to stuff up our town already.

ALEX: What are you here for?

PENNY: To tell you that we're about to rescind your option to buy the social housing land for your golf course.

ALEX: I wasn't going ahead with it in any case.

PENNY: Good.

ALEX: I miscalculated. The phone-sex thing worked for you, not against you.

PENNY: Maybe because just enough people are still basically decent. But mixing in your shark pool, you wouldn't meet any like that, would you?

ALEX: People like me have—

PENNY: Housed a lot of people and saved us a lot of carbon and become extremely wealthy doing it.

ALEX: So what are you really here to tell me? That I'm a horrible person? I know that and really quite enjoy it. It means I can say exactly what I think a hundred percent of the time. And that's brilliant.

Beat.

Seeing as you're here, I'll give you a little dose of reality in case you get too carried away with your victory. This country isn't about to become kind and gentle and fair just because you'd like it to be. We are a species defined by one overriding characteristic: ambition. Ambition for ourselves and our families, and nothing is ever going to change that. Money is always going to win out in the end.

PENNY: At least half-a-dozen people have told me they voted for me, even though your plan would've doubled their net worth, because they like the town as it is.

ALEX: There'll always be a few soft-heads. Most of us know there'll always be winners and losers and make sure they're winners.

She moves to the door and turns.

You've appointed Grace as your personal assistant?

PENNY: If she could cope with you, she could cope with anything.

ALEX: [*contemplative*] Nobody's ever got the better of me before. You're quality. If you ever want a job working for me, just call.

PENNY: That would be my number-one nightmare.

ALEX: Join the winners. I'd pay three times what you'll get here.

PENNY: Make that thirty times and I'll think about it.

ALEX *smiles and* PENNY *turns and walks out the door.*

Back in her own mayoral office, PENNY *strides in to see* GRACE *watching a news broadcast on the office television screen. The newsreader tells us that corporate profits have risen by record levels for the fourth quarter in a row but that food anxiety is now being suffered by three million Australian households. She turns the television off.*

We're going to move straight way on the four-storey height limit and we're going to really pressure the state government for seed money for social housing and we're going move on the short-term rental situation.

GRACE: Short-term rental. Tricky.

PENNY: I'm sick of big-city investors buying up our houses, making a fortune out of Airbnb'ing them, and driving up rents for locals.

GRACE: Ban short-term letting?

PENNY: Yes.

GRACE *raises her eyebrows.*

GRACE: Wow. There'll be very loud screams.

PENNY: Then it's about time we learned to stop flinching.

[*Turning in the direction of where* ALEX*'s hotel is*] Okay, Alex. You're right. Fairness is pretty much a lost cause in our sunburnt bloody county, our land of sweeping plains. But that battered old warhorse called democracy has handed me a chance to fight a bit of a rearguard action and by the ghost of bloody Ben Chifley I'm going to do it.

She turns to GRACE.

Okay by you, Grace? Take on the greedy shitheads?

GRACE *gives a thumbs-up.*

GRACE: Bloody oath!

They high-five each other and smile. Maybe it's only a temporary victory but they're going to try.

THE END

DAVID WILLIAMSON'S THE GREAT DIVIDE

DIRECTED BY MARK KILMURRY
ENSEMBLE THEATRE
8 MARCH 2024 – 27 APRIL 2024

Ensemble Theatre proudly acknowledges the Cammeraigal people of the Eora nation as customary owners of the land on which we work and share our stories. We pay our respects to Elders past and present.

CAST

CAITLIN BURLEY RACHEL POULTER
EMMA DIAZ PENNY POULTER
JAMES LUGTON BRIAN / JOEL
GEORGIE PARKER ALEX WHITTLE
KATE RAISON GRACE DELAHUNTY
JOHN WOOD ALAN BRIDGER

CREATIVES

PLAYWRIGHT DAVID WILLIAMSON AO
DIRECTOR MARK KILMURRY
ASSISTANT DIRECTOR JULIA ROBERTSON
SET & COSTUME DESIGNER JAMES BROWNE
LIGHTING DESIGNER VERONIQUE BENETT
SOUND DESIGNER DARYL WALLIS
STAGE MANAGER ERIN SHAW
ASSISTANT STAGE MANAGER ALEXIS WORTHING
COSTUME SUPERVISOR RENATA BESLIK

RUNNING TIME TWO HOURS (INCL. INTERVAL)
REC. AGES 14+
STRONG LANGUAGE, ADULT THEMES

The publication of this script was made possible by the generous support of Jenny Reynolds and Guy Reynolds AO.

Special thanks to Currency Press and Melanie Tait.

ENSEMBLE THEATRE

Ensemble Theatre is the longest continuously running professional theatre company in Australia and is committed to collaborating with exceptional playwrights and creative talent to present the best international plays, modern classics and new Australian works.

DIRECTOR'S NOTE

It is a real thrill to be directing David Williamson's first play out of retirement, THE GREAT DIVIDE. As usual, David has his finger on the pulse of what's current in Australian society and has created a play out of fear of losing the very things we cherish in our communities. Money talks and it takes real strength and courage to stand in its way—and perhaps personal sacrifice. This central conceit fuels THE GREAT DIVIDE and, as the title suggests, places opposing views within David's beautifully drawn characters.

It has been a real pleasure working with this fine, talented cast and creative team and I hope you enjoy this social comedy, which may also give rise to many lively conversations, long after the play has finished.

MARK KILMURRY
ARTISTIC DIRECTOR

WRITER'S NOTE

When I was a kid in the fifties, Australia was the second-most egalitarian country in the developed world. The difference in salary between a worker and a managing director seldom exceeded a factor of five. Now with Australia the third-least egalitarian country in the developed world, the ratio is more like a factor of 200. We are now the country of the Great Divide, where a minority enjoy a lifestyle of unimagined opulence and the rest of Australia can only look on, and the country in which most of the younger generation have been effectively locked out of home ownership for life. The efficient manner in which our neoliberal ideology, embraced by both our major parties, works to make the wealthy ever wealthier seemingly can't be stopped, certainly not by a playwright, but at least I can offer a glimpse of hope that suggests that occasionally, just occasionally, the seemingly inexorable power of money can be challenged by someone who is smart enough and angry enough to stand up against it.

DAVID WILLIAMSON AO
PLAYWRIGHT

DAVID WILLIAMSON AO
PLAYWRIGHT

Ensemble Theatre: Premieres include RHINESTONE REX AND MISS MONICA, CRUNCH TIME, THE BIG TIME, SORTING OUT RACHEL, ODD MAN OUT, JACK OF HEARTS, DREAM HOME, CRUISE CONTROL, HAPPINESS, WHEN DAD MARRIED FURY, NOTHING PERSONAL, AT ANY COST? (Co-written with Mohamed Khadra), LET THE SUNSHINE, LOTTE'S GIFT, OPERATOR, FLATFOOT (with Christine Dunstan Productions), A CONVERSATION, FACE TO FACE. Griffin Theatre Company: FAMILY VALUES. La Boite Theatre/ Noosa Long Weekend: STRINGS UNDER MY FINGERS. La Mama Theatre: CREDENTIALS, THE REMOVALISTS, THE COMING OF STORK. Melbourne Theatre Company: RUPERT, DON PARTIES ON, SCARLET O'HARA AT THE CRIMSON PARROT, BIRTHRIGHTS, SONS OF CAIN, THE CLUB, JUGGLERS THREE. Nimrod: CELLULOID HEROES, TRAVELLING NORTH. Old Tote: WHAT IF YOU DIED TOMORROW? Playbox: SANCTUARY. Pram Factory: DON'S PARTY. State Theatre Company South Australia: A HANDFUL OF FRIENDS, THE DEPARTMENT. Sydney Theatre Company: INFLUENCE, AMIGOS, SOULMATES, UP FOR GRABS (with Melbourne Theatre Company), THE GREAT MAN, CORPORATE VIBES (with Queensland Theatre Company), THIRD WORLD BLUES, HERETIC, DEAD WHITE MALES, SIREN, EMERALD CITY, THE PERFECTIONIST. Queensland Theatre Company: NEARER THE GODS, MANAGING CARMEN, AFTER THE BALL, BRILLIANT LIES, MONEY & FRIENDS. Film and TV include: FACE TO FACE, BALIBO, ON THE BEACH, BRILLIANT LIES, SANCTUARY, EMERALD CITY, TRAVELLING NORTH, THE PERFECTIONIST, THE LAST BASTION, PHAR LAP, THE YEAR OF LIVING DANGEROUSLY, GALLIPOLI, THE CLUB, DON'S

PARTY, ELIZA FRASER, THE REMOVALISTS, STORK. Awards: Some of David's many awards include twelve Australian Writers' Guild Awards, five Australian Film Institute Awards for Best Screenplay and, in 1996, the United Nations Association of Australia Media Peace Award. David has received four honorary doctorates and been made an Officer of the Order of Australia, as well as having been named one of Australia's Living National Treasures.

MARK KILMURRY
DIRECTOR

Ensemble Theatre: MIDNIGHT MURDER AT HAMLINGTON HALL, BENEFACTORS, RHINESTONE REX AND MISS MONICA, BOXING DAY BBQ, A DOLL'S HOUSE, THE WOMAN IN BLACK, OUTDATED, KENNY, CRUNCH TIME, THE ODD COUPLE, THE LAST WIFE, MURDER ON THE WIRELESS, THE BIG TIME, THE NORMAN CONQUESTS, SHIRLEY VALENTINE, TAKING STEPS, NEVILLE'S ISLAND, TWO, ODD MAN OUT, RELATIVELY SPEAKING, BAREFOOT IN THE PARK, BETRAYAL, GOOD PEOPLE, MY ZINC BED, EDUCATING RITA, ABSENT FRIENDS, OTHER DESERT CITIES, THE ANZAC PROJECT, RICHARD III, THE GLASS MENAGERIE, FRANKENSTEIN, MANAGING CARMEN, RED, THE SPEAR CARRIER and HAMLET. Film: Co-writer and co-director of BEING GAVIN. Literature Illustration: CAPTAIN COURAGEOUS. Awards: North Sydney Community Award.

JULIA ROBERTSON
ASSISTANT DIRECTOR

As Director; Little Eggs Collective: PINOCCHIO, RIME OF THE ANCIENT MARINER, EXTENDED PLAY: OLIVER SHERMACHER (with Sydney Recital Hall), METROPOLIS (with Hayes Theatre Co). Sydney Grammar School: RIME OF THE ANCIENT MARINER, JAMES AND THE GIANT PEACH. St. Vincent's College: MATILDA, THE SERVANT OF TWO MASTERS. Assistant Director; Joshua Robson Productions & Hayes Theatre Co: BONNIE AND CLYDE, CITY OF ANGELS. Actor; Belvoir 25A: JESS AND JOE FOREVER, THE ASTRAL PLANE, Christine Dunstan Productions: TIM, Griffin Theatre Company: WHEREVER SHE WANDERS, Little Eggs Collective: THE LOST BOYS, Sydney Theatre Company: THE REAL THING. Film: HOT MESS. Training: Lee Strasberg Institute of Theatre and Film (New York) and the Royal Academy of Dramatic Art (London).

CAITLIN BURLEY
RACHEL POULTER

THE GREAT DIVIDE marks Caitlin's debut with Ensemble Theatre. Belvoir St Theatre: OPENING NIGHT. Bell Shakespeare: ROMEO AND JULIET. Bell Players: 2020 and 2021. National Institute of Dramatic Art: A HAPPY NEW YEAR. Australian Theatre for Young People: INTERSECTION 2018: CHRYSALIS, OEDIPUS DOESN'T LIVE HERE ANYMORE. Cross-Pollinate Productions: EVERYBODY. Kings X Theatre: A GIRL IN A SCHOOL UNIFORM (WALKS INTO A BAR), AMERICAN BEAUTY SHOP. TV: TRICKY BUSINESS, AT HOME WITH JULIA.

EMMA DIAZ
PENNY POULTER

Ensemble Theatre: Play reading of David Williamson's TRAVELLING NORTH, Celebrating 50 years with David Williamson. Bell Shakespeare: HAMLET. Belvoir St Theatre: BLESSED UNION. Belvoir 25A: NEVER CLOSER. Monkey Baa Theatre Company: NAUTILUS, HITLER'S DAUGHTER. Sport for Jove: THE CRUCIBLE. Sydney Theatre Company: ON THE BEACH. Film: ISAAC'S DREAM, FRIENDS AND STRANGERS. TV: AFTER THE VERDICT, BUMP, PIECES OF HER, DIARY OF AN UBER DRIVER. Training: Western Australian Academy of Performing Arts Acting, Australian Film Television and Radio School Production Management. As a producer, Emma has worked with Belvoir St Theatre, Projector Films, Co-curious, ATYP, Kings X Theatre, Old Fitz Theatre and Acuity Films.

JAMES LUGTON
BRIAN / JOEL

Ensemble Theatre: A DOLL'S HOUSE, DIPLOMACY, THE ODD COUPLE. Bell Shakespeare: MACBETH, HAMLET, JULIUS CAESAR, OTHELLO, RICHARD III. Sport for Jove: THE HOLLOW CROWN, WAR OF THE ROSES, LOVE'S LABOUR'S LOST, THE IMPORTANCE OF BEING EARNEST, THE MERCHANT OF VENICE, THE CRUCIBLE, ALL'S WELL THAT ENDS WELL, MUCH ADO ABOUT NOTHING, CYRANO DE BERGERAC, HAMLET, THE TEMPEST, TWELFTH NIGHT, THE TAMING OF THE SHREW, MACBETH, THE LIBERTINE, AS YOU LIKE IT, ROMEO & JULIET, A MIDSUMMER NIGHT'S DREAM. Whitebox/Griffin Independent: UNHOLY GHOSTS. Monkey Baa Theatre Company: THURSDAY'S CHILD. TV: THE TWELVE, THE UNUSUAL SUSPECTS, DIARY OF AN UBER DRIVER, HARROW, DOCTOR DOCTOR, FIGHTING SEASON, MARY: THE MAKING OF A PRINCESS. Film: JOE CINQUE'S CONSOLATION, BMX BANDITS.

GEORGIE PARKER

ALEX WHITTLE

Ensemble Theatre: RHINESTONE REX AND MISS MONICA, MURDER ON THE WIRELESS, LUNA GALE, BAREFOOT IN THE PARK, RAPTURE BLISTER BURN, LET THE SUNSHINE, RABBIT HOLE, THEY'RE PLAYING OUR SONG, CHAPTER TWO. Footbridge Theatre and National tour: HOW TO SUCCEED IN BUSINESS WITHOUT REALLY TRYING, NUNSENSE. Marion St Theatre: WAIT UNTIL DARK, HERE COMES SHOWTIME. Queensland Theatre: THREEPENNY OPERA. Sydney Theatre Company: SCENES FROM A SEPARATION, ALL IN THE TIMING. Theatre Royal: CRAZY FOR YOU. Sydney Entertainment Centre and National tour: MAN FROM SNOWY RIVER. Film: THE 13TH SUMMER, THE STRANGER (short film) SANTA'S APPRENTICE (animation), IRRESISTIBLE, DANGER DOWN UNDER, YOUNG EINSTEIN, THE REPRISAL, THE BOY WHO HAD EVERYTHING, THE 13TH FLOOR. TV: HOME AND AWAY, PLAY SCHOOL, CITY HOMICIDE, SCORCHED, EMERALD FALLS, STUPID STUPID MAN, STEPFATHER OF THE BRIDE, THE SOCIETY MURDERS, ALL SAINTS, FIRE, OVER THE HILL, ACROPOLIS NOW, GP, ALL TOGETHER NOW, A COUNTRY PRACTICE, RAFFERTY'S RULES, BARLOW AND CHAMBERS. Awards: Georgie has been nominated for a Logie Award eleven times and won seven, two of them Gold for her television work.

KATE RAISON
GRACE DELAHUNTY

Ensemble Theatre: KILLING KATIE: CONFESSIONS OF A BOOKCLUB, TWO, THE GOOD DOCTOR, DARK VOYAGER, GINGERBREAD LADY, AT ANY COST?, NINETY, LET THE SUNSHINE, MARY STUART, STELLA BY STARLIGHT, CHARITABLE INTENT, CHAPTER TWO, BIRTHRIGHTS, AFTER THE BALL, ALARMS AND EXCURSIONS, WRONG FOR EACH OTHER, ROAD, A SHAYNA MAIDEL, MAN OF THE MOMENT, THE ADMAN and THE HEIDI CHRONICLES. Darlinghurst Theatre: TORCH SONG TRILOGY. Harvest Theatre Company, S.A: DAYLIGHT SAVING. Outhouse Theatre: HEROES OF THE FOURTH TURNING. Red Line Productions: THE SHADOW BOX. Valhalla Theatre: THE VAGINA MONOLOGUES for Adrian Bohm. Film: BEING GAVIN, GOING SANE, EBB TIDE, ENCOUNTERS, SUPERFIRE and CHECKPOINT. TV: A COUNTRY PRACTICE, E-STREET, HOME AND AWAY, PACIFIC DRIVE, OUTRIDERS, ALL SAINTS, F.A.R.S.C.A.P.E., NEIGHBOURS and MURDER CALL.

JOHN WOOD
ALAN BRIDGER

Ensemble Theatre: CRUNCH TIME. Lighthouse Theatre Company: SIGNAL DRIVER, A MIDSUMMER NIGHT'S DREAM, THE BLIND GIANT IS DANCING, NETHERWOOD, ROYAL SHOW, TWELFTH NIGHT. Melbourne Theatre Company: JUMPERS, ALL MY SONS, LAST OF THE KNUCKLEMEN, MOTHER COURAGE, SHINDIG, PLOUGH AND THE STARS. Melbourne Theatre Company/Sydney Theatre Company Hit Productions: THE CLUB. Nimrod: FLASH JIM VAUX, MEASURE FOR MEASURE, HAMLET ON ICE, ONYER MARX (Writer). Old Tote Theatre

Company: DEATH OF A SALESMAN, OEDIPUS REX, MAJOR BARBARA. Playbox Theatre Company Melbourne: A NIGHT IN THE ARMS OF RAELENE, COMEDIANS. Playbox Theatre Sydney: HAMLET. The Production Company: SHE LOVES YOU, NICE WORK. Queensland Theatre: THE TAMING OF THE SHREW, DIVING FOR PEARLS. State Theatre Company South Australia: LULU. Theatre Royal Sydney: CHESS THE MUSICAL, DIRTY ROTTEN SCOUNDRELS. TV: BLUE HEELERS, POWER WITHOUT GLORY, RAFFERTY'S RULES, THE TRUCKIES. Awards: Green Room Awards THE CLUB, It JUST STOPPED. Logies for POWER WITHOUT GLORY, RAFFERTY'S RULES. Gold Logie for BLUE HEELERS. John Wood has been a stalwart of the Australian Entertainment industry for 54 years starting at The Old Tote Theatre in Sydney in 1970.

JAMES BROWNE
SET & COSTUME DESIGNER

Crossroads Live: GREASE. Monkey Baa Theatre Company: YONG, JOSEPHINE WANTS TO DANCE and PETE THE SHEEP. CDP: TURNS, TIM, SPOT THE DOG. David Venn Enterprises: CRUEL INTENTIONS. Griffin Theatre Company: LADIES DAY, DIVING FOR PEARLS. Hayes Theatre Co: CABARET, XANADU. Joint Ventures: MIDNIGHT. Merrigong Theatre Company: LETTERS TO LINDY. Riverside's National Theatre of Parramatta: GUARDS AT THE TAJ. Sydney Opera House: VELVET, CIRQUE STRATOSPHERE and BLANC DE BLANC. Theatre Creation Japan: GHOST. Victorian Opera: THE SELFISH GIANT. Awards: Best Costume Design 2020 Broadway World Sydney Awards (Musical HAIR). Nominations in the Australian Production Design Awards, Green Room Awards and Sydney Theatre Awards. Training: Theatre Design at the Western Australian

Academy of Performing Arts and Australian Film Television and Radio School in Art Direction.

VERONIQUE BENETT
LIGHTING DESIGNER

Ensemble Theatre: THE MEMORY OF WATER, RHINESTONE REX AND MISS MONICA, A BROADCAST COUP, THE CARETAKER, A DOLL'S HOUSE, NEARER THE GODS (set and costume). Belvoir St Theatre: THE JUNGLE AND THE SEA, TELL ME I'M HERE, THE WOLVES. Circa: SACRE. Darlinghurst Theatre Company: NATASHA, PIERRE AND THE GREAT COMET OF 1912. Griffin Theatre Company: THE SMALLEST HOUR. Hayes Theatre Co: A LITTLE NIGHT MUSIC, THE LIFE OF US. Red Line Productions: BURN WITCH BURN, HAPPY DAYS, CHORUS, ANATOMY OF A SUICIDE, PERMISSION TO SPIN, HOWIE THE ROOKIE. Pinchgut Opera: PLEASURES OF VERSAILLES.

DARYL WALLIS
SOUND DESIGNER

Ensemble Theatre: MIDNIGHT MURDER AT HAMLINGTON HALL, MR BAILEY'S MINDER, A CHRISTMAS CAROL, RHINESTONE REX AND MISS MONICA, THE LAST FIVE YEARS, RICHARD III, FRANKENSTEIN and many more. Belvoir St Theatre: THE MAN FROM MUCKINUPIN. Circa: AURA, RECLAIMED PIANOS, ONE BEAUTIFUL THING, LANDSCAPE WITH MONSTERS. Hayes Theatre Co: HIGH SOCIETY. Merrigong Theatre Company: SOMETHING THAT HAPPENED, STRANGEWAYS CABARET, AS LUCK WOULD HAVE IT, THE SIRENS' RETURN, THE OUTSIDE MAN, THE AUROBINDO PROJECT. Milk Crate Theatre: FEARLESS. Monkey Baa Theatre Company: THE PEASANT PRINCE, FOX. Sydney

Theatre Company: WOMEN OF TROY. Cabaret: ELIANE MOREL, JACQUI DARK, THE STRANGE BEDFELLOWS, MITCHELL BUTEL, JENNY VULETIC, RUSS VICKERY. Ali & The Thieves: LEONARD COHEN KOANS, THE ROYAL SEED, LOU REED IN THE BARDO. Awards: Sydney Theatre Award Best Score and Sound Design (FRANKENSTEIN), Green Room Award Best Musical Direction (STRANGE BEDFELLOWS).

ERIN SHAW
STAGE MANAGER

Ensemble Theatre: MIDNIGHT MURDER AT HAMLINGTON HALL, SUMMER OF HAROLD, SUDDENLY LAST SUMMER, A CHRISTMAS CAROL, PHOTOGRAPH 51, UNQUALIFIED 2: STILL UNQUALIFIED, HONOUR, KENNY (plus tour), AN INTIMATE EVENING WITH PAUL CAPSIS, DIPLOMACY (plus tour) and FOLK. Australian Theatre for Young People: MOTH. The Old 505: LOVE, ME and LITTLE BORDERS. QPAC: BREAKING THE CASTLE. Sport for Jove: ROMEO & JULIET. Assistant Stage Manager: Ensemble Theatre: KILLING KATIE: CONFESSIONS OF A BOOKCLUB, BABY DOLL, THE NORMAN CONQUESTS, THE WIDOW UNPLUGGED OR AN ACTOR DEPLOYS and DIPLOMACY. Belvoir St Theatre: A ROOM OF ONE'S OWN and BLISS.

ALEXIS WORTHING
ASSISTANT STAGE MANAGER

Ensemble Theatre: THE MEMORY OF WATER, CLYDE'S, SUDDENLY LAST SUMMER. Australian Theatre for Young People: M.ROCK. Hayes Theatre Co: MURDER FOR TWO, NICE WORK IF YOU CAN GET IT. Neglected Musicals: BELLS ARE RINGING. PYT Fairfield: THE HEN HOUSE, National Institute of Dramatic Art: THE MAGIC FLUTE, FALSETTOS, JUST MACBETH, TALES FROM THE WILD BUSH, so/lo, WHEN THE RAIN STOPS FALLING.

RENATA BESLIK
COSTUME SUPERVISOR

Ensemble Theatre: THE MEMORY OF WATER, SUMMER OF HAROLD, MR BAILEY'S MINDER, BENEFACTORS, RHINESTONE REX AND MISS MONICA, CARETAKER, PHOTOGRAPH 51, THE ONE, OUTDATED, CRUNCH TIME, BABY DOLL, FULLY COMMITTED, FOLK, THE BIG TIME, LUNA GALE, SHIRLEY VALENTINE, THE KITCHEN SINK, BUYER AND CELLAR and many more. Bell Shakespeare: HENRY V, THE WINTER'S TALE, MACBETH. Belvoir St Theatre: FANGIRLS. New Theatricals: DARKNESS. National Institute of Dramatic Art: THE GOVERNMENT INSPECTOR, STAY HAPPY KEEP SMILING, THE TEMPEST, WOYCECK, A LIE OF THE MIND, PORT, THE THREESOME. Pinchgut Opera: RINALDO, MÉDÉE, ORONTEA, PLATÉE and many more. Sydney Festival: BETTY BLOKK-BUSTER RE-IMAGINED.

SUPPORT US

Every dollar counts. Ensemble relies on self-earned income to deliver all the programs that we do—commissioning new work, education outreach, producing world premieres, so please think about your capacity to make a gift to Ensemble. You can donate online at ensemble.com.au/support-us or contact Stephen Attfield, Philanthropy & Partnerships Manager, on **stephena@ensemble.com.au** or via **02 8918 3400**.

LIFE PATRONS

Those who have made significant contributions to Ensemble:

The Balnaves Foundation
Clitheroe Foundation
Jinnie & Ross Gavin
Ingrid Kaiser
Graham McConnochie
Neilson Foundation
Jenny Reynolds & Guy Reynolds AO
George & Diana Shirling

PLATINUM $20,000+

The Balnaves Foundation
Clitheroe Foundation
Ingrid Kaiser
Graham McConnochie
Neilson Foundation
Alicia Powell
Jenny Reynolds & Guy Reynolds AO
Southern Steel Group Pty Ltd
Christine Thomson

GOLD $10,000+

Diane Balnaves
Graham Bradley AM & Charlene Bradley
Darin Cooper Foundation
Jinnie & Ross Gavin
Steve & Julie Murphy
George & Diana Shirling
John & Diana Smythe Foundation
Jane Tham & Philip Maxwell

SILVER $5,000+

David Z Burger Foundation
Peter Eichhorn & Anne Willems
Friends of Tracey Trinder
James Family Charitable Foundation
Peter & Marion Lean
Val, Garry & Debbie
Merryn & Rod Pearse
Alan & Pauline Plumb
Annie & Graham Williams
Anonymous

BRONZE $1,000+

Michael Adena & Joanne Daly
Melanie & Michael America
Paul Bedbrook & Fiona Hopkins
Phil Breaden
Margaret Cassidy
Debby Cramer & Bill Caukill
Jayati & Bishnu Dutta
APS Foundation - Brent & Vicki Emmett Giving Fund
R J Furley
Jill & Tim Golledge
Alan Gunn
Andrew & Wendy Hamlin
Matilda Hartwell
The Hilmer Family Endowment
Michael Markiewicz
Barbara Osborne
Georgie Parker
Jim & Maggie Pritchitt
Ronald Sekel
Bob Taffel
Wendy Trevor-Jones
Dr Elizabeth A Watson
Gavin M. Wong
In memory of John & Vanda Wright
Anonymous x 2

COMMISSIONERS' CIRCLE

A group of like-minded Ensemble supporters who are passionate about storytelling and supporting artists to create new work for our stage.

Diane Balnaves
Graham Bradley AM & Charlene Bradley
Paul Clitheroe AM & Vicki Clitheroe
Jennifer Darin & Dennis Cooper
Ingrid Kaiser
Steve & Julie Murphy
Alicia Powell
Jenny Reynolds & Guy Reynolds AO
George & Diana Shirling
Jane Tham & Philip Maxwell
Christine Thomson

LEAVE A LEGACY

We would like to thank the following Estates for their generous donations:

Estate of Freddie Bluhm
Estate of Helen Gordon
Estate of Leo Mamontoff
Estates of Zika & Dimitry Nesteroff
Estate of Margaret Stenhouse

ENCORE CIRCLE

Thank you to the following people for bequests in their wills:

Mark Midwinter
Joe Sbarro
Anonymous x 7

Ensemble Theatre supporters are recognised for 12 months from the dates of donation. Current at 1 February 2024.

OUR PARTNERS

Thank you to our partners for playing a vital role in our success.

MAJOR PARTNER

ASSOCIATE PARTNER

STRATEGIC PARTNER

SUPPORTING PARTNERS

ENSEMBLE ED PARTNERS

ENSEMBLE THEATRE TEAM

Artistic Director **Mark Kilmurry**
Executive Director **Loretta Busby**
Chief Financial Officer **David Balfour Wright J.P.**
Senior Producer **Carly Pickard**
Associate Producer **Anna Williamson**
Literary Manager **Sarah Odillo Maher**
Casting and Events (Part-time) **Merran Regan**
Production Manager **Romy McKanna**
Deputy Production Manager **Paisley Williams**
Acting Technical Coordinator **Gints Karklins**
Resident Stage Manager **Lauren Tulloh**
Philanthropy and Partnerships Manager **Stephen Attfield**
Marketing Manager **Rachael McDonnell**
Deputy Marketing Manager **Charlotte Burgess**
Marketing Assistant **Emma Garden**
Junior Marketing Assistant **Osibi Akerejola**
In-house Designer **Cheryl Ward**
Media Relations **Kabuku PR**
Ticketing Services Manager **Spiros Hristias**
Ticketing and Office Coordinator **Sophia Egarhos**
Box Office Team **Osibi Akerejola, Mary Barakate, Angus Evans, Alishia Keane, Lauren Richardson & Kathryn Siely**
Accounts **Gita Sugiyanto**
Front of House Manager **Jim Birch**
Front of House Supervisors **Megan Cribb & Isabella Wellstead**
Head Chef **Ian Paul Aguilar Alarcon**
Restaurant Manager **Amy Mitchell**
Maintenance Coordinator **Paul Craig**

ENSEMBLE LIMITED BOARD

Chair Graham Bradley AM, John Bayley, Narelle Beattie, Mark Kilmurry, Anne-Marie McGinty & James Sherrard

ENSEMBLE FOUNDATION BOARD

Chair Paul Clitheroe AM, Diane Balnaves, Graham Bradley AM, Alison Cameron, Joanne Cunningham, Ross Gavin, Emma Hodgman, Mark Kilmurry & Margo Weston

ENSEMBLE AMBASSADORS

Todd McKenney, Brian Meegan, Georgie Parker & Kate Raison